That Place Called Home

TO SISTER FLORENCE
EDWARD KEARNEY—

Happy Birthday!

With warmest wishes,

Paul Grondahl

That Place
Called Home

A Very Special Love Story

Sister Mary Ann LoGiudice, R.S.M.
with Paul Grondahl

CHARIS

SERVANT PUBLICATIONS
ANN ARBOR, MICHIGAN

Charis Books is an imprint of Servant Publications especially designed to
serve Roman Catholics.

Servant Publications
P.O. Box 8617
Ann Arbor, MI 48107

Cover design: Eric Walljasper
Photographs and artwork courtesy of Sister Mary Ann LoGiudice.

00 01 02 03 10 9 8 7 6 5 4 3 2 1

Printed in the United States of America
ISBN 1-56955-201-0

LIBRARY OF CONGRESS CATALOGING-IN-PUBLICATION DATA

LoGiudice, Mary Ann.
     That place called home: a very special love story / by Sister Mary
   Ann LoGiudice, R.S.M; with Paul Grondahl.
        p.   cm.
     ISBN 1-56955-201-1 (alk. paper)
     1. LoGiudice, Mary Ann.   2. Mothers—New York (State)—
   Albany—Biography.   3. Nuns—New York (State)—Albany—Biography.
   4. LoGiudice, Barbara.   5. Adopted children—New York (State)—
   Albany—Biography.   6. HIV-positive persons—New York (State)—
   Albany—Biography.   7. Special needs adoption—New York (State)—
   Case Studies.   8. Mothers and daughters—Case studies.   I. Grondahl,
   Paul, 1959-II. Title.

   HV874.82.L64 A3 2000
   362.1'98929792—dc21
   [B]   00-035827

For Barbara

Contents

Acknowledgments

𝔊

With deep gratitude to God for the many blessings in my life, and for those people I especially wish to recognize for the love and support they've given me. I first thank my wonderful, close-knit Italian family, particularly my parents, who loved me unconditionally and instilled in me confidence, love, and respect for others, and for their lived example of caring for those who were lonely and less fortunate.

For my sister Mela and brother-in-law Art, my brother Joe and sister-in-law Mary. For their constant support, love, and care for Barbara, with special thanks to Mary and Joe, who were her surrogate grandparents for every school function. Also, thanks to my sister Connie and brother-in-law Joe, as well as my brother Sam and his friend Paul. Though they live a distance away, I was supported by their circle of love.

For my many nieces and nephews, who loved Barbara unconditionally, cared for her frequently, and did a lot of fun things with her, for which I'm most grateful.

For my dear friends, many of whom have known me all my adult life. For Father Chris DeGiovine, whom Barbara called every time a repair was needed in our home, or when she wanted some information about nature. For Father Tony Chiaramonte, who was Barbara's playmate and confidant, and who treated her as if she were his own child. For Helen Hayes, Marilyn Riley, Ronnie Herbst, Sister Anne Lawlor, and Sister Jane McCullough, who loved and accepted Barbara and made her part of our many dinners and celebrations. For Sister Kay Ryan, Betsy Rowe, Mary Jo Slowey, and Nancy Sandman, who loved and supported us through thick and thin, and for so many others who gave so freely of themselves to Barbara and me.

For the Sisters of Mercy, especially the Albany Regional community, who, by their individual and communal witness, have challenged me to grow and to serve those in need with tenderness and compassion. Special thanks to Sister Karen Marcil and her leadership team who were willing to be risk-takers in granting me permission to adopt Barbara, and to Sister Margaret Straney and the current leadership team who have been most supportive in making this book a reality.

For the staff at Community Maternity Services, who supported me throughout all my years with Barbara, especially for the group who loved and nurtured her and provided an on-site after-school program when she came to my office each day. They baby sat for her when she was well, and helped care for her during her final illness. I am most grateful to Kathleen O'Sullivan, Cathy Toedt, Tracie Killar, Mary DeCotis, Mary Lee Trudeau, Cathie Nailor, Peg Ellett, Jackie Buff, Sister Mary Margaret Hickey, and Mary Creighton, faithful friends to both of us.

For the staff at Farano Center who cared for Barbara in mind, body, and soul, especially Sue Van Alstine, Rose Thomas, Pam Irish, and Barbara's good friend, Sister Helen Moran, and all the other wonderful caregivers there.

For her caring and compassionate medical providers, especially Dr. Kallanna Manjunath, Dr. Nancy Wade, Mary Ellen Adams, Ray Oddy, and all the other staff at Albany Medical Center.

For the staff and faculty at Doane Stuart School, especially Sister Lucie Nordmann, Mary Lou McGurl, and Lisa Brown, who were enlightened about HIV and AIDS and welcomed and accepted Barbara. They respected her confidentiality and provided a safe, loving environment for learning.

For Barbara's companions at Cape Cod, Sister Maureen Joyce, Sister Penny Lynch, and Laetitia Rhatigan, who loved and entertained her during our vacations together.

For the Brothers at Weston Priory, for their loving acceptance of Barbara each fall and for their prayers and support for me during her illness and death. For my retreat group: Sisters Jane McCullough, Marie Matthews, Claude Ruehl, Helen Charles, Jane Silk, and Jeanne Snyder, who warmly welcomed Barbara into their lives.

For Sister Maureen Joyce, my friend and mentor, who gave me the courage to pursue adopting Barbara and who shared both the good times and difficult times.

For my friend Bishop Howard Hubbard, without whose guidance, wisdom, and support I would not have been able to make Barbara a part of my life.

For the Carlson family, especially June and Stella, who, with Amanda, shared in every aspect of our lives together and who provided support and understanding.

For Amanda, Barbara's friend and soulmate, who brought joy and love into both our lives.

For Barbara's friends, Dawn Moore and Richard Tracey, to her classmates at Doane Stuart, and to the many others who loved and nurtured her, too numerous to mention here, but who were part of her amazing journey.

And, most especially for Barbara, who continues to be an amazing gift in my life. In her few years she taught me profound lessons about life and death.

Sister Mary Ann LoGiudice

* * *

I would like to thank my editors at the Albany *Times Union*, where the story of Barbara and Sister Mary Ann, in a different form, was first published. In particular, I'm grateful for the support and encouragement of Jeff Cohen and Karen Potter, who helped nurture that earlier version, granted me a summer leave to write this book, and graciously welcomed me back to the newspaper after I took a brief detour from the work of telling the human stories I love best. There are too many friends and colleagues at the paper to thank individually, but they've been a kind of second family to me the past fifteen years and I appreciate their good humor and enduring friendship.

Thanks to Daniel Mandel, a thoughtful and patient literary agent whose belief in the beauty of this story never wavered. Thanks also to Bert Ghezzi, Heidi Hess Saxton, and Helen Motter, editors at Servant Publications, caring professionals who helped improve the manuscript and made the process a pleasurable one.

Collaborating on this story of finding a family and making a home reinforced for me how special my own family is. I thank my parents, Ken and Bonnie Grondahl, and my brothers, Gary and Dave, for their love, encouragement, and support. I count myself doubly blessed with the kindness and generous spirit of my extended family, my wife's parents, Jack and Charlotte O'Donnell, and her siblings, Ann, Sheila, John, and Tim, as well as their partners.

Finally, to my wife, Mary, and my children, Sam and Caroline, I offer my heartfelt gratitude for bringing to my life so much joy and happiness and for embodying the lessons of love, family, and home that are at the core of this book.

Paul Grondahl

Foreword

⸙

God's blessings come to us as unexpected gifts. We can't anticipate them. And we can't demand them. They simply are. And if we have an open heart and embrace that mystery, it can change and enrich our lives in powerful ways.

That was how a little girl named Barbara became the adopted daughter of Sister Mary Ann LoGiudice, a Roman Catholic nun and member of the Sisters of Mercy. It took perseverance and a strong will to convince her religious order and the Catholic Church to allow this unusual arrangement. In the end, it felt like it was meant to be. Divine fate, if you will.

As both a Sister of Mercy and a single mother, Sister Mary Ann broke new ground for women in religious life. But that was never her motivation. Barbara needed a mother, which was something Sister Mary Ann had longed to become. More simply, Sister Mary Ann fell in love with a remarkable child who taught her more about spirituality and being a good Catholic than any theology textbook ever could.

Together, Barbara and Sister Mary Ann undertook a journey of the heart and formed a family. Like any deep and lasting relationship, their joyful union was tinged with difficult circumstances and its abiding faith was tested by disease and the fear of one's mortality.

Barbara arrived in Sister Mary Ann's life with more pain and tragedy than any child should have to endure. Her birth mother was terribly sick with full-blown AIDS and would soon pass away. The biological father she never knew was in prison and would eventually die from AIDS, too. Barbara had nobody else to call a family. She was essentially orphaned, and under the care of county social services workers.

That's when God's blessing showed up one winter night in a fuzzy pink blanket sleeper, clutching a Raggedy Ann doll. Barbara and Sister Mary Ann made each other whole. They shared a profound love and joy together.

The extraordinary connection that developed between mother and daughter described here teaches us many important lessons that are as much about the universal human experience as they are about any particular religious tradition. It's true that Barbara's indomitable spirit revived and deepened Sister Mary Ann's own spiritual search. That was a happy byproduct of their relationship. But neither set out to reach that conclusion.

The time that Barbara and Sister Mary Ann shared as mother and daughter was, unfortunately, brief in years, but it was long and rich in the things that matter—like the love and strength of family.

And the comfort and support of loving another and being loved in return. And how risking pain to experience indescribable joy is a worthwhile chance to take.

Barbara's story continues to resonate and offer lessons about love and spirituality, about racial harmony, and about compassion for people with HIV and AIDS.

Barbara touched many lives and she is honored in numerous ways. A tree planted by her classmates grows tall and strong. Money donated in her name brings toys and the fun of field trips to children with special needs. An AIDS display for Barbara and her best friend, Amanda, travels around the country, reminding us of the plight of babies born with AIDS. These commemorations are powerful educational tools in an ongoing effort to remove the stigma, while increasing understanding and empathy, for the children diagnosed with HIV and AIDS.

And when God's blessings arrive in your life, without any warning, it is my hope that you will be open to them, embracing the unexpected with a caring heart and a belief in the mystery of the sublime. And remembering a child named Barbara, who left a legacy as beautiful and inexplicable as the emergence from their cocoons of the yellow butterflies she so loved.

Eunice Kennedy Shriver

Introduction

ℐᔑ

A s I sat in the semidarkness of the theater, waiting for the movie to begin, I felt for a moment as if I were watching a film of my life. Scenes spooled out in my mind's eye, flickering images that sparked powerful recollections before they quickly dissolved and were replaced by a vague feeling of loss. There was the sound of my father's voice, its cadences still those of his Sicilian boyhood, calling out a friendly hello to a customer at our family grocery store in Albany, New York. I remembered the way sunlight streamed through the stained-glass windows as colorful shafts of light that washed over me and infused me with the presence of God as I prayed in the chapel during my novitiate at the Sisters of Mercy convent. One of the strongest memories was the touch of my daughter's soft, fine hair on my cheek as I cradled her in my arms and rocked her to sleep at night, humming a lullaby.

So many images scrolled fleetingly through my consciousness, as if they were the final credits at the end of a film. I wanted to slow down these fragments of my past, to hold on to these memories, to make them last, and to never let them fade away.

I had come to accept, however, that we don't get to choose how our story turns out. I know in my heart that God has a plan for us. This certainty is the foundation of my faith, even during the difficult times when I have questioned that faith and lost my trust in the restorative power of redemption.

These thoughts unleashed a torrent of emotions as I gazed at the little girls seated in the row just ahead of me—especially Barbara, who had come into my life unexpectedly and changed it in ways I never imagined.

Barbara and Amanda huddled together in the front row of the movie theater in the manner that eight-year-old girls who are also best friends do. They leaned in close to each other, shoulder to shoulder, head resting on head, white skin and black skin melded into one. They clutched each other's hands like they never intended to let go, as if they could freeze this instant and never let anyone or anything take its joy away from them.

It was a Saturday matinee and the theater was nearly empty. As we entered, I told the girls they could choose any seat they wished, but they didn't hear me. They both made a beeline for the front row, direct center. Their giggles of anticipation filled the theater as they scrunched down into their seats.

We had come for *Homeward Bound*, a movie Barbara and Amanda had been asking me to bring them to see for weeks. I kept finding excuses to put off the trip but finally relented when nurses and doctors encouraged the outing. They said it would probably do more good than anything the medical profession could provide at that point for either girl. When I said they could go to the movie, you could see their excitement, their eyes bright and happy and showing the first glimmer of hope after months of illness and growing despair.

The chance of the girls achieving a full recovery, or anything even approaching a cure, had already faded. In the end I'd decided to bring them to the movie just to let them enjoy a few moments of joy and escapist pleasure. That was the best I could offer.

Barbara and Amanda had been inseparable from the day they first met as preschoolers. Even in the hospital they demanded—and received—adjoining rooms and unlimited visitation back and forth. As I watched them sitting there in the front row, sharing a bucket of buttered popcorn and a large Coca-Cola, I could hear the two bubbling over with whispered laughter. They were electric and shining in the cool darkness, full of vitality and possibility. You could imagine their lives at the beginning of a long road bright with promise, like the opening shot of a movie.

In the dusky half light of the theater, you couldn't tell from behind how sick both girls really were. Barbara had lost so much weight she was practically skeletal, all jutting bones and loose flesh, barely able to stand or walk on her own. Nothing the doctors tried up to this point had been very successful, neither the central line feeding tube for malnutrition nor the intravenous fluids for dehydration. The long list of medications prescribed to combat days of high fever and a lung infection gave little relief. The diarrhea and vomiting, meanwhile, remained virtually constant for Barbara. By comparison Amanda seemed almost fortunate—if you consider losing your eyesight lucky, that is. Amanda's main symptom was blindness. Otherwise she was feeling tolerable for now. It was all relative, of course.

"OK, Amanda, shhh! Shhh! It's starting." Barbara acted as the guiding eyes for her best friend and offered a running commentary. Amanda intently faced the screen as she listened.

"It's called *Homeward Bound: The Incredible Journey*," Barbara told Amanda. Barbara liked being the commentator and in charge and proceeded to explain the plot to Amanda.

The movie tells a story about the animals belonging to three children in a newly created blended family. Chance was an orphaned terrier-mix puppy the family had adopted from the pound. Shadow was a loyal old golden retriever. Sassy was a smart-aleck cat who lived up to her name.

The action occurs when the family has to move. They temporarily leave their pets with a friend who lives on a farm, but fearful of being abandoned, Chance, Shadow, and Sassy flee and set out to find their family and return home. Their quest turns into a long and perilous journey.

"What's happening? What's happening now?" Amanda asked.

Barbara tried to keep up her play-by-play. "They're lost in the woods," she said. "It's dark and rainy ... they're hungry ... they've got to cross a river ... a bear's growling at them ... it's getting scary," she told Amanda. "Oh, no. Sassy just fell into the river and got swept over a waterfall ... they can't save her.... Chance and Shadow are looking for their friend, but she's gone ... they can't find her, so now they have to go on without her.

"There's a big, scary mountain lion after them," Barbara went on. "They're running away ... they made it ... but Chance got hit by a porcupine in the nose."

"Is Sassy really dead?" Amanda asked.

"Wait. Wait. She's alive. They're all back together again," Barbara said.

"They're all going to be OK, aren't they?" Amanda asked. "They're going to find their family? Make it home?"

"Yeah, they'll make it," Barbara said. She turned and hugged Amanda. "They're going to make it home."

In the end, that's all that really matters, I've come to learn. Barbara helped teach me that important lesson. That's all any of us wants, isn't it? To find our family. To make it to that place called home. To complete the trip safe and sound and perhaps to find redemption.

Watching Barbara and Amanda enthralled with *Homeward Bound*, I thought about the incredible journey of these two girls. Both were orphans. Neither had really known her biological father. Both were brought to a place far from where they were born and what would have been home if there had been someone there to care for them. As it turned out, they were taken into the care of social workers, raised by nurses and other hired strangers, and then made available for adoption.

I sat next to June Carlson, Amanda's adoptive mother, in the second row, just behind Barbara and Amanda. June and I both dabbed tissues at moist eyes during the ending of the movie. Barbara was right, after all. They found their family and made it back home, safe and sound. The voice of Chance, the orphan dog who had been adopted, could be heard summing up the story at the end of the movie: "A new feeling came over me. I had a family. At last, for the first time in my life, I was home."

The credits finished, the lights came up in the theater, and I knelt to lift Barbara into my arms to carry her to the car. She called me "Mommy" and gave me a hug. I called her "honey" and squeezed her back.

Barbara is my daughter. I am a Roman Catholic sister, a member of the Sisters of Mercy of the Americas religious order. I adopted Barbara; the titles "sister" and "mother" both describe me. I broke new ground for women in religious life, but I consider myself a supporting character in the story of this incredible journey.

Barbara is the central figure, the heart and soul of the narrative. A tiny waif, a mere slip of a girl, Barbara never weighed more than forty pounds, even when she was healthy. She drifted into my world like an autumn leaf carried on the wind and transformed me, my family, and a community of friends with her extraordinary life force and amazing grace.

Amanda's mother, June, and I shared the joys and sorrows of raising these two special girls who were best friends. We both knew from the start that these girls had HIV, the virus that leads to AIDS, and, at least in those days, so often resulted in death. As mothers we both struggled with when we would tell our daughters they had the virus.

Yet we approached each day with our daughters as a

blessing. Because of these little girls, we were able to form families that were unexpected gifts. I was a sister and never thought I'd have a chance to be a mother. Neither did June, a single woman who lived with her mother when she adopted Amanda. As we became mothers to Barbara and Amanda, we knew pain and sadness lay ahead, but we focused on the traveling itself rather than the destination.

I wish Barbara could offer her own running commentary of her life the way she helped the sightless Amanda "see" the movie. Barbara would tell her story better than I can. It would be full of humor and silly nonsense jokes told in her high, bright, squeaky voice. The events would be viewed through a child's eyes, all innocence and optimism. But since Barbara can't tell it herself, I'll try.

This book is about a journey, a daughter's and a mother's, and the lessons learned along the way. It is about finding family in the most unforeseen places and ultimately about trying to get home. Even when home is someplace you never imagined.

Chapter One

A Search for Vocation

B arbara arrived at Farano House in Albany, New York, when she was three years old. County social-service agency workers pulled up outside late on a snowy January night after a two-hour drive north with their tiny passenger. Barbara, dressed in a fuzzy pink zippered blanket sleeper, had fallen asleep in the car clutching a teddy bear and a Raggedy Ann doll. A social worker gently carried her up the snowy steps and into the Colonial-style house that was to become her home. Barbara had no place else to go.

Her mother, in the final stages of AIDS (acquired immune deficiency syndrome), was in the hospital, and her biological father, a man Barbara had never known, was in prison. The foster family who had expressed interest in Barbara withdrew their offer when they learned she was infected with HIV (human immunodeficiency virus).

This was 1988. Little was known about how the virus was contracted or spread. Without sufficient facts and too often hearing misinformation, the public was afraid. Babies like Barbara who were born to HIV-infected mothers (or those who already had full-blown AIDS) were often shunned, the least fortunate condemned to hospital back wards, innocent victims of public fear. A caring community of people in New York State's capital city had formed to offer comfort to children like Barbara.

In 1986 Sister Maureen Joyce, a member of the Sisters of Mercy and director of Community Maternity Services (CMS) in Albany, the Reverend Michael Farano, chancellor of the Albany Roman Catholic Diocese, and I visited a hospital in a desperately poor inner-city neighborhood of New York City. A pediatrician invited us back to an out-of-the-way wing. The babies we found there, the doctor told us, were ones nobody wanted because they had been diagnosed with HIV.

I'll never forget what the pediatrician told us. "These babies will live and die in this hospital," she said. "Nobody will take them."

The situation had attracted the attention of New York City tabloid newspapers, which had run stories about "the boarder baby crisis." Despite the sensationalistic coverage, nobody appeared to be stepping forward with concrete ideas for addressing the problem.

Sister Maureen and Father Farano were tremendously moved by the desperate situation, and so was I. We returned to Albany committed to trying to provide some help for these beautiful but unwanted babies. Perhaps it was more than coincidence when, just a few days later, a "For Sale" sign went up on the house next door to my office at CMS. Father Farano wasted no time in negotiating its purchase. "I always sensed that it was meant to be" was how Sister Maureen put it.

In the fall of 1987, the Albany Roman Catholic diocese celebrated the official opening of Farano House, three months before Barbara arrived. As the first licensed residence in New York for HIV-positive children, it became a model for the state and the nation. The house provided a refuge and homelike atmosphere for these babies and young children that nobody else seemed to want. Barbara was among the first ten to arrive.

Farano House became part of CMS, a ministry of Catholic Charities. I was hired by Sister Maureen Joyce to help there and eventually became director of CMS, a job title that makes me friend, mentor, and surrogate parent to pregnant teens, as well as an administrator. We sum up our work with a simple saying, written on a sign that hangs in the kitchen of one our houses: "If It Cries … Love It."

My job has also given me the privilege and responsibility of coaching dozens of teenage girls through labor and delivery. I never grow tired of witnessing the miracle of childbirth.

My staff and I then work with the young mothers to teach them necessary parenting skills before they leave the CMS fold. Our hope is to get them and their babies off to a good start and, with each new beginning, to break the cycle of neglect and abuse. Some have said our work on North Main Avenue makes it "the Avenue of Promise."

Within our row of five homes on North Main, we experience the entire cycle of life: babies are born, teenage girls become mothers, infants are nurtured, and children occasionally are buried. If you don't believe in potential and promise, you don't work here. We have our share of trials and tribulations, believe me, but it is an overwhelmingly hopeful place, where young women with damaged souls begin to heal.

Each year we serve more than eight hundred pregnant teens and teen mothers, plus dozens of HIV-positive children. And every day we try to take to heart the words of Catherine McAuley, founder of the Sisters of Mercy: "In the care of the sick, great tenderness above all things."

I have always found my work at CMS fulfilling and still do, even after more than two decades. Yet it can also be enormously challenging—at times even a source of despair, particularly when I observe the same cycle of family dysfunction repeated again and again.

A CMS staff person hung this quotation on the wall in a satellite office: "Remembered joy can break the heart. But who in the darkest moments would miss the joy?" That speaks well to my experience here, but sometimes the sharp turns of emotion leave me feeling downcast and anxious.

January 1988—one month away from my fortieth birthday—found me in just such a dark mood. I began having doubts about my work and vocation, and started to question seriously my role in religious life. These were not new uncertainties; for months I had been analyzing my past and pondering my future as a sister.

I grew up on Watervliet Avenue in Albany's West End, the youngest of five children. I'm Italian on both sides of my family, which is reflected in my looks: olive skin, dark brown hair, and brown eyes that can narrow and flare with a quick temper. At least that's what I'm told by my friends, who also remind me that my laugh comes just as easily, deep and loud, revealing a gap in my top front teeth. I learned to use my hands a lot when I talk. I'm part of a large, extended Italian family, after all, and when we get together there are two volumes: loud and louder. The hands never get a rest.

My father, Santo LoGiudice, was born in 1896 in Sicily and at age eighteen came to America to make a better life. He ended up in upstate New York, where he had relatives, and worked as a laborer, digging canals and working on other large construction projects.

My mother came to the United States with her mother from Naples when she was just two years old. My parents met in Albany, courted, married, and established a grocery store in the city's West End, Sam's Cash Market. My father never shied away from hard work; in his early years in Albany he did two jobs simultaneously: driving a taxi and working in a grocery store. As the years went by, he had plenty of mouths to feed: Connie, Joe, Carmela, Santo, and me.

Born in 1948, I was the baby of my family, surprising my parents twelve years after the birth of their second youngest child, who was named after my father. There was a span of twenty-three years between my oldest sibling, Connie, and me.

Our kitchen and dining room were behind the family store, with living quarters upstairs. Sam's Cash Market, with its striped green awning out front, was located on Watervliet Avenue, in a working-class neighborhood dominated by Irish-Catholics who walked to work at the nearby West Albany shops of the New York Central Railroad. I was enrolled in the neighborhood parochial school, Blessed Sacrament School, and we attended Blessed Sacrament Church.

Sam's—named after my father, whose nickname was Sam—was well known for its meat market. My dad was the butcher and was said to make the best Italian sausage in the city. We ate well. And when times were tough, especially during the Depression, the neighbors could always count on coming to my dad and receiving groceries on credit.

Our family had a regular Sunday ritual. First we went to Mass and then to Saint Agnes Cemetery to visit the graves of relatives. The day would culminate in a big Italian supper presided over by the family matriarch, my maternal grandmother, Carmela Vigliucci. We ate in the dining room behind the store, and our meals were continuously interrupted by the tinkle of the bell on the front door, meaning a customer had entered the store. My dad prided himself on staying open seven days a week and accepted these Sunday-meal interruptions as just part of running his own business. He was almost seventy before he finally gave in to our requests and closed the store for thirty minutes during Sunday supper so we could eat in peace.

LoGiudice gatherings always resounded with the gleeful noises of youth. There were many children in our extended family, and I never wanted for playmates growing up. When my sister Mela married and moved in next door, it meant our family gatherings would come to include even more of the life on Watervliet Avenue.

Mine was a happy childhood, with the usual mischief and occasional acting-out in the mix. I had the nickname Mimi, or Mim, and I tried to live up to the joyful sound of that. I didn't look for trouble, but it knew where to find me. As a youngster I certainly wasn't a pious, goody two-shoes—nothing resembling the common stereotypes about girls who grow up to be sisters.

There's never a dull moment for a kid growing up in a grocery store. Sam's Cash Market was my family's livelihood and the center of my parents' life—and, by extension, their children's universe, too. And it helped to have five children and numerous nieces and nephews when you ran a grocery store, where there is always much to do. We all were assigned jobs. Mine was to stock shelves, though as I got older, my role shifted to baby-sitting nieces, nephews, and cousins.

My dad's workday began before sunrise at the Menands Farmer's Market, where he was known to be a tough negotiator when selecting the day's produce. The store itself was open from seven in the morning to eleven at night, seven days a week. My father even extended store hours for an extra half-hour during holiday seasons at the request of people who worked the late shift at nearby King's department store.

Mom's sweetness and her welcoming nature with our customers offset Dad's exterior gruffness. She was known far and wide as the proprietor of the best penny-candy display cases in town. Kids came from all over to my mom's candy counter, and they got a lesson in proper manners in the bargain. My mom always insisted that they say "please" and "thank you" when making a candy purchase.

My dad was usually in the back of the store, taking care of supplies, or behind the meat counter in his blood-spattered butcher's apron, preparing cuts for a steady stream of customers. When business was slow, he'd go through the kitchen and dining room and into our backyard, where he coaxed from an urban patch of soil the most surprisingly delectable tomatoes, cherries, peaches, figs, and other fruits and vegetables.

He loved his garden. I was never much for digging in the dirt and preferred instead to sit inside, behind the checkout counter, where I could chat with the neighbors who passed through. As the baby, I was the spoiled one who often got a reprieve from the toughest chores. But I helped stock shelves, made grocery deliveries, and visited sick and elderly relatives and neighbors.

My mom was forever making up boxes of meals for our neighborhood's shut-ins, and I was the emissary for her Good Samaritan ways. I liked how it made me feel to see an old woman's face light up and how she praised my mom's kindness as I dropped off the food. A vague sense of calling to devote my life to a ministry of service—already beginning to stir in me during adolescence—surely grew out of Mom's spirit of generosity.

From my dad, I learned about running a small business. Several, actually. In addition to the grocery store, he owned rental properties on Watervliet Avenue and a couple of brownstone apartments across town. He was firm as a landlord and drove a hard bargain in business, but it wasn't affluence that motivated him. We continued to live above the grocery store, where our lifestyle was solidly working class. It was more that my dad liked running things, making them work, and investing the extra income with his five children in the form of private education, music lessons, and the like. And yet I will always remember his compassion when the poor and hungry came to our store asking for food. My dad treated them with respect and kindness and always gave them free groceries. He told me, "Never let them go away hungry."

My mother, a devout Catholic, named me for the Virgin Mother and her own mother. My father did not share her religious ways and essentially boycotted going to church other than for weddings and funerals, Christmas and Easter. But though outwardly stern, my father was a profoundly kind and caring man who helped the less fortunate without calling attention to his acts of kindness. And even though I was especially close to him, we didn't talk about religion.

He did support my Catholic education, however. After completing eight grades at Blessed Sacrament, I entered Vincentian Institute High School, also run by the Sisters of Mercy.

These sisters deeply impressed me during my school years, and it was their influence that led me to begin seriously thinking while I was in high school about becoming a sister. It's hard to explain, but somehow, deep inside me, I felt a stirring of faith, a calling to a religious vocation. Shortly after high school graduation, I made up my mind to enter the Sisters of Mercy. The convent was only a few miles from the store, and better still, my best friend from

Blessed Sacrament decided to enter along with me.

I was afraid to tell my parents at first but couldn't keep the news from them for long. I had anticipated their reactions. My mother was excited; my father was upset. The notion of me in a convent was at odds with my dad's notion of my getting married and raising many children, continuing the family tradition of large, boisterous gatherings for Sunday suppers and trips to the cemetery. It was just expected of a LoGiudice, after all. One of my sisters had six children and a brother had five. That's the way it was done in my family.

My father finally gave me an ultimatum: if I entered the convent, I was abandoning my family duties and he would not come to see me anymore. He was serious. I felt banished.

I could still hear my father's admonishment echoing in my head when at age seventeen I apprehensively entered religious life with the Sisters of Mercy. After the exuberance of my extended family's Sunday gatherings and the communal ebb and flow of the grocery store, I wasn't prepared for the culture shock of the convent. Although it was located only about three miles from home, it felt as though I were living a world away.

As postulants our day began at dawn. We first participated in morning prayers; then early Mass, which was followed by breakfast. Like all other meals, this was eaten in silence. We then prayed or meditated throughout the day. Occasionally we were allowed to leave the convent walls, and overall our rules were less stringent than in cloistered orders. Still, we wore long black skirts and black blouses and were given little freedom. The toughest part of convent life for me was the strictly enforced silence.

For quite some time I was terribly homesick. I longed for my family, my friends, the store, the steady stream of children from the neighborhood, our Sunday rituals. My transition was eased somewhat by my best friend, Barbara Wood, who had entered the convent at the same time. We'd been practically inseparable since fourth grade.

What helped me most during that long, often lonely first year was the return of my dad. The prodigal father. He eventually ignored his earlier decree and came to visit me as often as convent rules allowed, which was one Sunday per month for a few hours. He didn't change his mind, however, about my having made a foolish choice, and he shared with me his indifference to organized religion.

He also told me a secret. Before I was born, to appease my mother, he used to tell my older brothers and sisters that he daily attended 6:00 A.M. Mass, as a way of explaining his absences at church on Sundays. Now he admitted that was all a ruse. He shared a lot of stories, and we laughed often during those precious visits. We both cried when he had to leave.

In 1968 I was twenty years old and not yet finished with my novitiate when my father died at the age of seventy-two. This painful loss made me feel even more alone and homesick. Eighteen young women had entered the convent along with me; ten dropped out before final vows. As each friend quit, more doubts rose in my mind about religious life. Barbara remained, however, and was a valuable support. I like to think that in return I helped her stick it out through our novitiate, although she too eventually left religious life.

I stayed on with the Sisters of Mercy and earned my associate's degree at Maria College, which is adjacent to the convent and run by our order. Later I earned a bachelor's degree in elementary education at the College of Saint Rose in Albany, my sister Carmela's alma mater.

Once trained, I taught second grade and also worked at summer day camps with inner-city children, most of whom were mired in poverty. I felt confined in the parochial grade school, but the social-work aspect of helping children in Albany's inner city was invigorating and deeply rewarding. Later I also worked with women who were released from prison to a halfway house. That, too, felt like important and satisfying work.

But something was missing. It wasn't anything as obvious as a lack of material comforts, although I'll admit it was difficult at first to make peace with a vow of poverty and a stipend of twenty-five dollars per month. I couldn't fully articulate the lack of wholeness I felt, but a sense of emptiness clung to me.

The pull of family and children and several generations around a table for Sunday supper did not vanish when I entered the convent. If anything, that tug grew stronger over the years, and I felt the familial yearning more than ever as I settled into the routines of religious life. I was Aunt Mimi, after all, to the five daughters of my brother Joe and his wife, Mary. I loved to baby-sit the quintet, and they returned my affection. In fact, they'd argue over who got to sit next to me at the table for holidays and family gatherings. I imagined myself as a mother to the one niece with whom I had developed a particularly strong bond.

Meanwhile my superiors were pushing me to make the

ultimate commitment, final vows. I had been putting them off, seeking extensions, but now was my moment of truth. A decade had passed since I entered the convent in September 1965. It was high time to decide.

In June of 1975 doubts still swirled around in my head. I had watched my best friend leave religious life, along with several other of my contemporaries from the convent. Finally I too decided to quit. Suddenly, after a decade as a sister, I was just Mary Ann LoGiudice again.

I knew what I was leaving—or thought I did—but what was I moving toward? I was twenty-seven years old when I left the Sisters of Mercy. I wasn't bitter at all about the experience. I had tried it, had grown, and had learned some valuable lessons. But in the end, I decided that a lifelong commitment to that life was just not for me. Leaving the religious community meant another transition, though, and I experienced a fair amount of anxiety about heading out in an uncertain direction.

Both my parents were dead by now—my mother passed away in 1972—and I felt a new sense of aloneness. Part of that stemmed from the loss of our family center, the store. After my dad died, Mom couldn't handle all the details of the business and closed the store, though she continued to live in the apartment above it.

When Mom died, we decided to sell the building. That was the end of an era in the LoGiudice clan; our parents' apartment had been the center of our universe. Now the store was gone along with my parents, and all that we cherished had faded away. I had plenty of family members left, of course, but they had established their own careers and lives and families. Meanwhile I was starting over and just beginning to discover a direction amid my newfound freedom.

My sisters, brothers, nieces, and nephews supported my decision to leave religious life and offered their assistance in helping me find an apartment. I quickly got hired at a day-care center in Albany's inner city, where I felt I could go beyond teaching and make a difference in these often grim young lives.

During this period I also lived and worked for two years at Arbor House, a halfway house for teen runaways, women released from prison and psychiatric centers, battered women, recovering alcoholics, and drug addicts. Our clients were, in short, the kind of women society had given up on. Arbor House was located in a crime-ridden area of the inner city.

Sharing this work with me was Ronnie Herbst, still a Sister of Mercy at that time. Ronnie remembers scenes from Arbor House much more vividly than I do. She reminded me recently of a frantic call I made to her when I discovered girls growing marijuana on a windowsill of the third floor. The police found the pot at the same time and took the girls away in handcuffs. With Ronnie's help, we bailed out the girls and got them off with just probation. We also had girls who suffered psychotic episodes and threatened suicide. I learned how to negotiate the mental health system and how intake works at the local psychiatric center. We had pimps ringing our doorbell, looking for young women who used to work as prostitutes for them. I broke up my share of fights, including wrestling a knife away from a woman who brandished the weapon after hiding it under her wig. As director, I assigned Ronnie the toughest tasks, including the extermination of cockroaches, mice, and rats.

Some of the situations were truly scary, and I shed several layers of naiveté at Arbor House. I made a lifelong friend, though, in Ronnie, who for a time shared an apartment with me. She now conducts educational training for St. Peter's Hospital in Albany—another Sisters of Mercy institution—and we've remained close over many years, career shifts, and life changes.

After leaving the Sisters of Mercy, I also started dating. I could still hear my father's voice in my head, encouraging me to marry and be happy (and multiply, of course). My plan was clear, as obvious as the traditional path my siblings had followed. I wanted to meet the right man, settle down, get married, and have children. I envisioned a big family, a continuation of how I was raised.

Years earlier, while still in the convent, I had met a man through my sister Carmela. He had followed my progress from afar by talking to my sister, and after I left the convent, we reconnected. Mike was a teacher. We felt an immediate attraction, and a strong bond developed as we dated. We shared common values and goals, and we both wanted children. In addition to this strong foundation, we were giddy with the excitement of new love. Our relationship also had the blessing of my family; they really liked Mike and were happy for us.

After two years of dating and ongoing discussions about our future together, Mike was ready to make a commitment. He was a wonderful man and I loved him, but I still somehow felt unfulfilled. It was a vague apprehension, a sense that my life was meant to take a different turn.

It was a difficult period. I felt pulled in opposite directions, and I prayed for guidance, meditated, and spent many hours alone. Finally I came to terms with what I had been contemplating for some time: a return to religious life. It took a lot of soul-searching to give voice to this deep stirring to be a Sister of Mercy once again.

I felt awful for Mike. He had talked about buying an engagement ring, and I knew he planned to propose soon. I've always struggled with making these fork-in-the-road life decisions and have usually found solace in procrastinating. I knew my defining moment loomed. It wasn't fair to Mike to continue, so I broke off our relationship in the winter of 1979. Mike was extraordinarily kind and understanding.

My family wasn't. My brothers and sisters didn't take the news nearly as well as Mike did. They couldn't believe I was doing this. After coming to know and respect Mike, they had considered our marriage a foregone conclusion. Even now, twenty years after the fact, I can't fully explain my reversal, other than to acknowledge that I was a walking advertisement for the cliché "God works in mysterious ways."

In 1980 I officially became *Sister* Mary Ann LoGiudice once again. This meant another moving day, too; I gave up my apartment and went back to a tiny room in the Sisters of Mercy convent. And on March 7, 1981, I embraced the ultimate commitment I had so long avoided, taking my order's final vows: poverty, chastity, obedience, and service to the poor, sick, and ignorant. Mike came to the ceremony. I loved him all the more for that gesture of kindness.

The Mass and ceremony are very much like a wedding. I received a ring, a simple silver band that symbolized a union with Jesus Christ and my commitment to religious life. The inscription I chose for my ring comes from one of Saint Paul's letters: "Let love be the root and foundation of your life."

Chapter Two

Barbara's Captivating Presence

I've often thought of my life and Barbara's as two planets circling each other in their own orbits, drawn together by a powerful and beneficent force. Call it God's will, or any other term you like. But the way in which the two of us connected was more than mere coincidence. It's hard to imagine such a union without the hand of a divine presence at work.

It so happened I was working at CMS that snowy night of January 27, 1988, when Barbara arrived at Farano House, which is across the street from my office. Social workers brought Barbara up from Putnam County, a couple of hours south of Albany. The little girl's mother was hospitalized with severe complications from AIDS, and no other facilities in downstate New York would accept an HIV-positive child. Barbara was classified as an "emergency placement" and brought to Farano House, a kind of last resort for children like her. The county social workers helped Barbara get settled into a crib, completed their paperwork, and left. Barbara slept.

It was around 10:00 P.M. when my phone rang. I was still in my office, finishing up a report. It was Sister Maureen Joyce, my boss at CMS and also my friend, whom I'd known from the convent and my work at the halfway house for released prison inmates. Maureen was my mentor. She was four years ahead of me in the convent and showed a big sister's concern. She had hired me at CMS during my hiatus from the Sisters of Mercy and was wonderfully supportive during that difficult and confusing time in my life.

Maureen's voice couldn't contain her excitement over the phone. She told me there was a beautiful little girl who had just been dropped off at Farano House. "You've got to come over and look at her before you go home tonight," Maureen said. "She's so sweet." I was tired, it was late, and I was blessed with more cute nieces and nephews than any aunt could hope for. All the soft spots in my heart for sweet little children were filled through my doting on nieces and nephews. But Maureen was adamant. I respected her opinion, and besides, she was my boss and her request had the tone of an order. I wrapped up my work and walked across the street.

I wasn't prepared for what I saw and felt. I can't explain the glow of joy that seemed to wash across me. Barbara was so cute and peaceful in her crib. She had auburn hair cut in a pageboy style, and her cheeks were chubby and rosy. Some of the young children arrived appearing thin and sickly, but Barbara looked wonderfully healthy and exuded a sense of vitality. She was sound asleep, sucking her thumb, the image of a sweet little cherub. I was smitten with my nieces and nephews and spent all the time I could with them. But this felt like a different connection from the beginning, something deeper and more astonishing.

Farano House is yellow, a soft lemony hue. It has high dormers and a steep roof. Later Barbara came to think of the dormers as wings and the house as a yellow butterfly. As she got older, she drew pictures of yellow butterflies. They were peaceful and happy drawings. From this first glimpse of Barbara in her crib, I could see that she felt safe in her new home. In the ensuing years, she would continue to feel safe and sound in the yellow butterfly house.

The day following her arrival, I walked over to Farano House after work, which I often did on my way home. Barbara was awake, and she zeroed in on me as soon as I came through the door. Her self-confidence astounded me, considering she'd been there less than twenty-four hours. She already acted as if she owned the place. I'd never seen a child adjust so quickly to new surroundings. Barbara went into the dining room with the other children, who were getting ready to eat dinner.

I do not wear a habit but dress in regular clothing and often wear jewelry. That day I was wearing a big, thick bangle bracelet that was shiny and gold-colored. I hadn't even been introduced to Barbara at this point, but she took a shine to my bracelet and asked if she could wear it. I took it off and gave it to the little girl, but instead of sliding it onto her three-year-old wrist, she placed the bracelet atop her head like a crown.

A very serious look, almost a scowl, crossed Barbara's face as she tried to assume the look of royalty. "I'm the queen," she said. "And you're the princess. We live in a big castle. There's a purple dragon that protects us." Barbara carried on about the castle, informing me that we were safe from all evil as long as we stayed inside. Outside, she warned me, there were bad things.

I was spellbound by this bright and precocious little pixie. She was so verbal, and her eyes danced in a mesmerizing shimmer of energy. Barbara's eyes were the shape of almonds and seemed deep and knowing, with a wisdom beyond her years. They were the color of emeralds and they captivated me. There was so much life and energy in this wise little presence. She had an upper tooth that jutted out a bit, causing her lip to curl when she grinned. Her smile and laughter could brighten any room.

I wasn't planning to stay for dinner that night, but Barbara told me to sit next to her at the table. It wasn't a request. I learned right away that she liked to give orders. Being bossy came naturally to her, yet she did it in a way that was endearing rather than obnoxious. So I stayed and we ate macaroni and cheese—what else?

After dinner, the little girl asked in her wispy voice if she could keep the bracelet. I said she could borrow it for the night. It was still perched on her head at this point, the head of Queen Barbara. "Your Highness," I said, nodding in deference and telling her I would return tomorrow and would get the bracelet back then. Barbara bid me goodbye and informed me that she was a good queen with special powers. She told me once again to be careful outside the castle, where there were evil things. All this coming from a three-year-old child.

I was spellbound and couldn't get her out of my head. The staff and volunteers at Farano House told me the same thing. Unlike most other children, who arrived fearful and tentative, and remained teary-eyed or silent for their first days of transition in the new setting, Barbara acted like an old-timer on her first day.

She entertained herself—as well as the other children and the staff—with a vast repertoire of nursery rhymes delivered in a giggly, singsong torrent of words. As she measured out her rhymes about the cat and the fiddle, the mouse who ran up the clock, three men in a tub, and more, Barbara's thin, short legs dangled over the edge of a dining room chair and kept the beat with a metronome's precision. Her black patent-leather shoes caught the light in rhythmic flashes. She was also a whiz at knock-knock jokes. She repeated the old standards but showed remarkable inventiveness for a three-year-old in creating her own. Most of her original compositions were nonsensical, but that hardly mattered. She laughed at the sound of them anyway, and her giggle proved infectious among her captive listeners.

The following day after work, I again walked over to Farano House, this time with the intention of staying for dinner and engaging Barbara in conversation. She told me to sit right beside her, close, shoulder to shoulder. She didn't offer the bracelet. I didn't ask for it. The thing was cheap enough, and I figured after what she'd been through, the least I could do was let her keep the trinket and be queen for more than a day. That evening we ate spaghetti. Barbara picked at her food.

After dinner I stuck around as I sometimes did to help the

staff get the children ready for bed. Barbara gave the orders again. She informed me she wanted me to give her a bath. Nobody else would do. I complied with the command and afterward zipped Barbara into her freshly laundered fuzzy pink blanket sleeper. She was as light and airy as a cloud.

Earlier that day, her second at Farano House, Barbara had been assigned a new room—her very own—at the top of the stairs. To her delight, the room was painted light purple, the color of her imaginary dragon. It had a big window with a clear view of the street. There she could watch people walking past on the sidewalk below. Barbara liked to observe the passersby, and if one glanced up at her, she would wave. She told me more than once that she liked having her own room and was happy she didn't have to share it with anyone else.

That evening Barbara asked me to read her a bedtime story. I got a book and sat in the wooden rocking chair in her room. She clutched her Raggedy Ann doll and snuggled into my lap. After I had read two books, Barbara was still awake. She didn't want to go to sleep, she told me; she wanted to talk to me.

"I miss my mommy very much," Barbara said.

I paused and didn't speak, but I felt my face flush and a lump rise in my throat. I searched for the right words. "I'm sure your mommy misses you very much, too," I said. "Do you think she's OK?"

"She's in the hospital," Barbara said. "People don't go into the hospital unless they're pretty sick." Earlier in the day she had talked to her mother's caseworker, Adrian. Adrian had told her that her mommy sent her love and wanted to let her know she was doing all right.

I lifted Barbara into her crib, above which were wall hangings of Bambi, Thumper, and Flower. Barbara still wasn't ready for sleep, so I told her a little story about each character. She was so smart that in moments she had memorized every story. I turned out the lights and said it was time to go to sleep. Then I softly kissed her good night on her forehead and tiptoed out of the room. The floorboards creaked.

A little voice came out of the darkness. "Will you hold my hand until I go to sleep?" Barbara asked.

She asked me to sing her a song too, so I sang her lullabies. The little girl's breathing became soft and light, like the rustle of tall grass. Her hand was damp and continued to grip mine tightly. I gently freed my hand and eased across the floor once more. Barbara woke up and started crying. "I'm afraid," she said through sobs. "Please stay with me." I held her hand once more, stroked her hair, and hummed a soothing melody. After a long time, she finally fell sound asleep.

On that night, in that room with Barbara, lulled by the comfort of the dark and quiet, holding the hand of a sweet innocent with nowhere else to call home, something deep inside me felt at peace. It was as if I had found my true calling, had finally acknowledged the maternal longing I had felt keenly and deeply for so long. It had always been there, an ache of absence. Baby-sitting nieces and nephews was fulfilling, but it only lasted for a short time and then they returned to their parents. Already, after just a few hours with Barbara, I experienced how she filled up those empty places within me as nobody else ever had. The little girl was an unexpected gift. There was nowhere else I wanted to be for dinner except beside Barbara. Nowhere else I would rather be at night when it was Barbara's bedtime. Barbara was the queen and I was the princess of her castle, after all. I couldn't express this in so many words at that moment, but I knew my life had been irrevocably changed and a special and profound bond had begun to form between us on those first few nights together.

Soon the dinners and bedtime routines with Barbara weren't enough. I began finding excuses to walk across the street to Farano House in the morning and again in the afternoon. Nobody believed my pretenses after a while, either, as the staff members quickly realized what was going on. Sister Maureen, mentor and friend, encouraged my special bonding with this delightful little girl. Barbara was bright and intuitive and verbal, and on some level, I believe, she realized she needed someone to take care of her like a mother because her own mom no longer could.

For myself, I realized I longed to love a child as if she were my daughter, which was something I never anticipated being able to experience as a sister. In the end I discovered that it's true what they say in social-work circles. I didn't adopt Barbara. She adopted me.

Chapter Three

A Child in Need

Barbara arrived in my life as inexplicably as a dream, full of mystery and wonderment. It was uplifting to experience the powerful emotion of feeling connected to this sweet child on some deep level. The harsh realities of Barbara's difficult background and grim circumstances would come crashing down soon enough, though, shattering the reverie.

I didn't know many details of Barbara's history, but I pieced together bits of background over time. Her mother's name was Angeline. Angeline had been born and raised in Yonkers, New York, as an only child. Her childhood was strained. Her mother, Barbara's grandmother, was mentally ill and had been confined to a mental institution since the time Angeline was a young girl. For most of her childhood, Angeline was raised in foster homes. Her father was not around, and her stepfather was only a vague presence in her life.

I learned that, despite her difficult circumstances, Angeline was bright and hard-working. She would not give up her dream of a better life. She earned a high-school equivalency diploma and was selected for a job training program. She received public assistance but deeply wanted to find a job in order to get off welfare. And for a time, she did make it on her own.

Then she met Wayne, a handsome and charming young man. They were both in their early twenties at the time and soon began dating. It didn't take long for Angeline to fall in love with Wayne, and they eventually moved in together. Their early courtship was sunny and bright, and Wayne made Angeline feel special and needed—something she hadn't experienced much growing up. Soon enough, though, Wayne's dark and dangerous side began to surface. Shortly after he had moved in with Angeline, his heroin addiction became evident. He stole, forged checks, and dealt drugs to pay for his habit. His behavior was erratic and his outbursts scared Angeline. Still, she longed for companionship and the promise of a happily-ever-after future she felt marriage to Wayne might offer her.

Wayne did not marry Angeline, but he did get her pregnant. Then he was sentenced on charges stemming from drug dealing and check forgery and was sent away to prison for a long time. But not before he had gotten his pregnant girlfriend hooked on heroin, too. It was likely they shared unsterile needles when injecting the drug.

For her unborn daughter's sake, Angeline vowed to kick her heroin addiction and checked herself into a drug rehabilitation clinic. She was pregnant and alone, more afraid than she had ever been. But her desire to prove herself a fit mother was stronger than the lure of the narcotics. Angeline battled her addiction and set out on a course of recovery. She successfully completed treatment and had just been released from rehab when Barbara was born on August 18, 1984.

Barbara was born prematurely and weighed just three pounds, eleven ounces. Angeline did not know at this point that she had HIV. She was unaware, too, that she had passed the virus on to her daughter; neither mother nor daughter was tested after delivery for the virus that leads to AIDS.

As a premature infant, Barbara needed to spend weeks in the hospital while her condition was monitored. She slowly gained weight and strength from a special diet and was released from the hospital. Angeline was twenty-four years old and had no experience and few examples from her own childhood about how to be a loving and nurturing mother. She faced other problems and challenges, too. She was homeless and unemployed, with no immediate job prospects. Her mother remained in a mental institution, and neither her biological father nor stepfather was in the picture. Wayne, her boyfriend and Barbara's biological father, was still in prison and slowly succumbing to AIDS. Although he had been abusive and was responsible for her heroin addiction, Wayne was the only family Angeline had to build a future around, and she wanted Barbara to see her father, even if Barbara was too young to have any memory of the encounter.

The brief prison visit was one of the last times all three members of this family, such as it was, would be together. Angeline's health declined, and she spent increasing amounts of time in the hospital. Visiting Wayne in prison provided some closure for her. She broke off their relationship shortly afterward, telling him she was getting her life in order and didn't want him interfering any longer.

Despite strong pride and her desire to become independent of the welfare system, Angeline knew her situation was desperate, and she reached out for help. Putnam County social workers took a liking to Angeline and her baby and gave their case special attention. They secured welfare benefits and arranged for the two to stay in a private room at a welfare hotel. The accommodations weren't great, but Angeline had lived in worse places. At least mother and daughter were together, and although it was just a one-bedroom unit, they had a home of their own for the first time.

As part of her drug treatment, Angeline continued to attend meetings and receive counseling at the rehab facility. That's where she met Dennis, a resident in the rehab program. The courtship wasn't as intense and mercurial as that with Wayne, but the relationship slowly took hold and deepened. Angeline, who had remained clean and sober, got a job and began a savings account.

She was good at stretching a dollar, and by the time Barbara was about a year old, Angeline had saved enough money to rent a home. She found a conveniently located and affordable rental, a blue house in Carmel—also in New York's Putnam County—where she lived with her daughter until Barbara was three years old.

Barbara liked to tell stories about her time there and had happy memories of the blue house. But the house turned dark and menacing, as Barbara recalled it, when Dennis was drinking. She said that Dennis—who lived with them in the blue house for a time—was mean when he drank.

Angeline, no stranger to addiction, knew what she had to do to protect herself and her daughter. She ended the relationship but let Barbara continue to believe that Dennis was her father, knowing Barbara would benefit from feeling she had the stability of a dad in her life.

There is a photo of Angeline, Dennis, and Barbara at the child's baptism in a Catholic church in 1984. Dennis is tall and thin and appears awkward and uncomfortable in a three-piece suit, long arms hanging uncertainly at his sides. Angeline is petite and dark, with a small, round face and delicate features. She's smiling and looks radiant in a white dress, her dark, shoulder-length hair pulled straight back. She is holding Barbara, who is wearing a white, lacy christening outfit and sucking on her fingers, grinning for the photographer. It is the picture of contentment, at least for the momentary click of the camera shutter. The truth behind the photo was a far different image.

The social workers familiar with her case praised Angeline's skills as a single parent. Despite the difficulties she had endured and a lack of parenting models growing up, Angeline worked hard at being a good mother. Barbara's room was tidy and filled with books, stuffed animals, and other toys. Jars of baby food were arranged just so in the kitchen. Angeline kept a scrapbook devoted to Barbara and dutifully recorded memorable events and minute increments of her child's early development. She doted on her little girl and enjoyed dressing her up like a doll—all frilly outfits and lacy accessories.

Angeline's declining health brought out a need in her to

explore many avenues of spiritual expression, especially any church that promised relief from pain and suffering. One of the churches Angeline began attending was a fundamentalist Christian congregation that promoted faith healing. Angeline became deeply involved in the church and developed a friendship with the minister and his wife.

As she became sicker, Angeline discussed her concerns about Barbara's future care with the couple. They assured Angeline that everything would be taken care of and that they would adopt Barbara. The three together drew up an adoption plan, and all the details appeared to be in place to ensure Barbara's well-being.

Then, as efforts were made to diagnose Angeline's deteriorating condition, new tests showed that not only did she have HIV, but it had now advanced to full-blown AIDS. Angeline's first response was to get her daughter tested immediately for HIV. Barbara tested positive. Keeping that information from her daughter, Angeline discussed the results and health implications with the minister and his wife. They didn't know much about HIV and AIDS—only what little they had read in the popular press—but it terrified them. They withdrew their adoption offer. When Angeline got too sick to care for her daughter, Barbara was referred to the Putnam County social workers. And subsequently she came to us at Farano House.

Angeline's diagnosis was *pneumocystis carinii pneumonia*, along with multiple other respiratory ailments and intestinal problems associated with AIDS. She improved slightly during an extended hospital stay and pleaded with doctors to be discharged so she could see Barbara.

In February 1988 Angeline was released from the hospital for a reunion with her daughter, and Barbara was brought downstate for a visit. Their reunion lasted just three weeks. Then Angeline's symptoms got worse and she had to be re-admitted to the hospital. She and Barbara made what would prove to be their last goodbyes, and Barbara was returned to Farano House on the third of March.

Sixteen days later, on Friday, March 19, Barbara's mother died. Barbara was in Albany, her biological father was in prison, and Angeline's stepfather—whose involvement in her life was sporadic and marginal—made hasty burial arrangements.

On Monday the staff at Farano House was informed that Barbara's mother had died and had already been buried. It was their job to break the news to the little girl, who was now three and a half years old. I knew Barbara felt most comfortable with me, so I offered to talk with her. I'll never forget our exchange.

"Your mommy was very sick, Barbara," I said.

"Yeah, she could hardly get out of bed," she replied. "That made me sad. But my mommy still loves me lots."

"Your mommy was in a lot of pain," I told her. "She couldn't breathe. Sometimes when people are very sick like that, no matter how hard the doctors try and how much medicine they give, they just can't make those people better."

"You mean my mommy died and went to heaven?"

"Yes, that's right, Barbara. Your mommy died and went to heaven."

"Does that mean I won't see my mommy anymore?"

"That's right," I said. "You won't be able to see your

mommy anymore. But she's no longer in any pain. And she'll always watch over you."

"My mommy must be really sad in heaven that she won't be able to see me anymore."

I felt my throat go tight with emotion and knew I'd catch on my words if I tried to speak. I didn't disturb the heavy silence. I reached out and stroked Barbara's soft, fine hair and felt her lean in toward my touch. Nothing in my background or training prepared me for trying to help a young child cope with death and grief. I knew Barbara would need to talk about this again, and I had no idea how to answer her probing and difficult questions. Even though she was so young, not yet four years old, Barbara possessed a remarkable, intuitive wisdom about love, loss, and matters of the heart. I would let her be the guide and follow her lead through this emotional and difficult terrain.

I knew this much: I would speak the truth to Barbara and would never lie to her about the unpleasant realities of illness and death if asked. I struggled with how much information I should volunteer. In the end, I believed Barbara deserved not only my love but also my honesty, and I knew that walking that fine line would mean learning how to view the world from a child's perspective.

Chapter Four

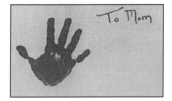

Looking for a Mother

The spring of 1988 was a dark and difficult time for Barbara. Following her mother's death, she refused to eat and became withdrawn and sullen. She resumed wetting the bed, sucked her thumb continuously, and regressed in other ways. Her grief was palpable, and she seemed deeply depressed. She argued and fought with other children at Farano House, acted out, threw tantrums, and fell into long crying jags. The staff struggled to help and tried to encourage her to discuss her grief, but nothing seemed to work.

I thought a change of pace might help, so I started taking Barbara on special lunch outings. She had always enjoyed this one-on-one attention, but all she did now was cry and say how much she missed her mommy. All I could do was wait for Barbara to work through her grief. I listened, held her hands, let her rest her head on my shoulder—and waited.

Weeks passed and little changed. I hoped that at least time would bring healing.

One day, as we left for lunch, Barbara looked up to the sky and out of the blue asked me, "Is that where heaven is? Do you think my mommy is sitting on that cloud looking down on me?"

I assured Barbara that her mother was watching over her always.

She followed up that question with another, one that caught me off guard. She said she wanted to throw her mommy a birthday party and asked if I'd help. She added that she only wanted to invite people who believed her mommy was in heaven. That was fine by me, I said.

I helped Barbara with the party preparations. She picked the day for the birthday celebration at random. On the chosen day, her invited guests arrived. They were mostly priests and sisters, friends of mine who had taken a personal interest in Barbara. Father Chris DeGiovine, Sister Helen Moran, Father Tony Chiaramonte, Sister Maureen Joyce, and Bishop Howard Hubbard were on Barbara's approved list. They all showed up for the unusual party, even the bishop.

Barbara had decorated her room at Farano House with balloons. I brought a cake. Barbara had fashioned a gravestone for her mother out of construction paper. (I had taken her to visit her mother's grave at the cemetery a few weeks before, and she was very concerned that it didn't have a proper gravestone.) The paper gravestone said "Angeline" on it, with construction-paper tulips and grass growing along the side. Barbara made her homemade gravestone the centerpiece of the birthday party. She carefully arranged all the photographs she had of her mother around the gravestone. Barbara showed the snapshots to her guests and told them stories about her mommy, about the blue house in Carmel, about seeing her mommy sick and in the hospital, about what she thought it was like in heaven where her mommy lived.

The party turned out just the way Barbara had hoped. She was elated. After the bishop and other guests thanked her for inviting them to the party and left, I remained with Barbara in her room. She seemed at peace, her old self again. It struck me then that Barbara had just given her mother a wake and a memorial service. The simple ritual brought healing to Barbara and offered the closure she craved.

After her birthday party for her mommy in heaven, Barbara's depression quickly lifted, and the outgoing and vivacious little girl we had known returned. A sense of springtime was restored in her life, and she radiated a bright and sunny sense of purpose.

As Barbara's fourth birthday approached, the Putnam County social workers were wanting to find her a permanent foster home. Farano House was only meant to be a temporary refuge for abandoned HIV-infected babies, a gateway to placement in foster care, and hopefully, adoption. The Farano staff interviewed and screened potential foster parents for Barbara.

I remember in particular a single woman in her forties from western New York who expressed interest in becoming a foster parent to Barbara. After she had applied and passed the review process, she was informed that the child was HIV-positive. Unlike others who backed away after learning of Barbara's medical diagnosis, this woman was not dissuaded.

She came to Albany to meet Barbara. This was standard

protocol, a chance to see if there was compatibility and a sense of chemistry between the child and potential adoptive parent. It was quickly apparent they were not *simpatico*.

For starters, the woman was a chain smoker. Barbara hated cigarettes and told the woman so. The woman was also quite rigid and stern. Again Barbara spoke her mind freely and often about what she deemed unpleasant traits in the woman. Their meeting got off to a rocky start and became worse as it went along.

Barbara was a free-spirited girl who told silly nonsense stories, sang with gusto, and laughed loudly. Her idol was Goofy, the Disney character, and she cultivated a cartoonish giddiness and tried to be just like him. The woman did not share Barbara's sense of humor or accept her choice of Goofy as a role model.

One night they went out to eat at the Ponderosa buffet. Barbara didn't want to go, so she invited me to come along. I tried to resist, but the woman decided she could use reinforcement and Barbara got her way. The meal was a disaster. Barbara refused to sit next to the woman and basically ignored her throughout dinner. Barbara hardly touched her food, and the only thing she really wanted to do was to make her own ice-cream sundae. The woman told Barbara she couldn't have ice cream until she first ate her dinner like a proper young lady. That sent Barbara into a tantrum. She screamed, threw herself on the floor, and flailed her fists and feet while letting loose with paint-peeling shrieks.

The woman beat a hasty retreat from the restaurant. Barbara had just quieted down when the woman's rules about the car ride home set her off again. She wanted to ride in back with me. The woman told her she had to ride in front. Barbara screamed some more and kicked and punched her car seat all the way back to Farano House. She could put on an all-star performance when it came to being stubborn.

Despite the ordeal of dinner, the woman was not ready to withdraw her application. She decided she wanted her trial session with Barbara to continue. Here was the main event: stubborn versus more stubborn, a battle of wills. I kept my thoughts to myself as the woman insisted on going through with the next phase, which was to have Barbara spend a weekend at her house. As soon as Barbara heard that, she dug in her little heels. She said she wouldn't go.

Despite her fuss, there was nothing for the Farano House staff to do but to tell Barbara she had no choice on this one. Their efforts to convince her it would be fun were feeble, and she wasn't buying it. Even though her fourth birthday was still several weeks away, she was extremely bright and intuitive and had already learned how to play staff members off each other. She came to me and asked if I could do something to call off this visit.

"I want to stay with you, Sister Mary Ann," she said.

I had to tell her, "I'm sorry, but you can't. You have to go, Barbara. And I'm sure you'll have a lot of fun once you get settled in there."

I didn't sound convincing at all. I imagined a scene like the one at dinner stretched out over a weekend. However, it would be out of line for me to intercede and try to get the trip canceled. Instead I brought a small gift for Barbara—a tiny ceramic beaver trinket she had seen in my office and had said she liked.

"Take it with you on the trip and keep it in your pocket," I told her. "If you're sad or lonely, you can take it out of your pocket, look at it, and you'll know I'll be thinking of you and that I love you very much."

I promised Barbara I'd see her again in a few days when she returned to Farano House. I gave her a quick hug and said it was time to go. The woman was waiting in her car. I walked Barbara to the curb, helped her in, gave a little wave, and walked back into my office. I didn't let her see my tears as she left in the woman's car for the long drive west.

I kept wondering and worrying how the visit was going and couldn't focus on anything else that weekend. I resisted the urge to call and ask to speak with Barbara. That would be unprofessional. I had an answer sooner than expected. Barbara did not make it through the weekend. A Farano staff member had to drive out to bring her back after just one night because it wasn't working out and the woman was frustrated.

The woman was angry and demanded that she be allowed to try for another weekend. It was that rigidity and sternness again, the attributes that had soured Barbara on the woman during their initial meeting at dinner. I didn't voice my opinion, but I was secretly pleased when the staff at Farano House decided a match between Barbara and the woman was not meant to be. End of tryout. Case closed. At last.

Meanwhile, the issue of Barbara's placement was back to square one. Her legal guardians, the social-services officials of Putnam County, were more anxious than ever to find a foster match for Barbara. She had been living at Farano House for five months, and the staff had run out of leads for adoptive parents. Barbara's options were stalled. I'd been dreaming about a farfetched notion but kept it to myself. It was too unrealistic.

I couldn't keep this notion inside forever, though, and spoke to my closest friend, Sister Maureen Joyce. It felt good to talk about it, to give voice for the first time to what I had felt in my heart since that first night I'd read bedtime stories to Barbara and soothed the frightened child. Maureen, my mentor and boss, had a way of making me get to the point.

"If I weren't in religious life, I would apply to be Barbara's foster parent," I said.

I expected Maureen to tell me to forget about it, but she was encouraging. She told me I had nothing to lose by exploring the possibility with my superiors in the Sisters of Mercy. She told me to schedule a meeting right away.

I figured Maureen was just being a friend and laughed off her suggestion as absurd. But she had planted a seed in my mind and it took root. I sought the advice of other friends. To my surprise, another Sister of Mercy, Jane McCullough, thought the whole idea was an amazing opportunity to break new ground for religious life, and she said I should go for it.

Farano House director Sue Van Alstine didn't even wait for me to ask her opinion. She said I'd be great as Barbara's foster mother, and she said the rest of the staff thought so, too. Nobody would be a better choice, she insisted.

This encouragement had me floating with excitement, but I needed to be brought back to the ground. I sought out Father Chris DeGiovine, a good and faithful friend whose pragmatism and directness I valued. He listened as I went on and on about my dreams for a life with Barbara.

Eventually, Father Chris spoke. He was supportive, but he also thought I was a bit naive about what I was getting myself into. He asked some penetrating questions. In particular he asked if I had thought this all through—not just the fact that I was a sister seeking to be a mother, but the fact that Barbara had grave health concerns and special needs. Could I really continue to excel at my demanding and difficult full-time job, remain an active participant in my religious community, and raise a daughter—one with HIV besides?

Father Chris articulated the same concerns I harbored, although I had felt so needed by Barbara that I had looked beyond any misgivings. Nothing was resolved.

I returned to my routine of work and visiting Barbara for dinner at Farano House, but I could not let go of the crazy notion and had a difficult time sleeping during that period. Part of the reason was that I had turned forty years old recently and felt the need to take stock and meditate on where I had been, where I was going, and how I should be trying to fulfill God's plan for me. I lay awake at night thinking of my childhood and our big Italian family. I thought of our rituals and of baby-sitting my nieces and nephews. I remembered leaving religious life and falling in love with Mike, my longing to be a mother, and my returning to the Sisters of Mercy and continuing my career as Sister Mary Ann. Nothing could compare to the overwhelming connection I felt to this little girl.

Barbara consumed my thoughts. I couldn't imagine her going off to live with somebody else and my never seeing her again. I finally admitted to myself that I was in love with her and that she loved me and that this was the deepest and most powerful emotion I had ever felt. I had always longed to be a mother, and a mother was what Barbara desperately needed. The match had been made. It seemed like it was meant to be, as if all the pieces of the puzzle were just waiting to be joined together. But many obstacles lay ahead.

Chapter Five

Religious Life and Maternal Longing

I took my good friend Sister Maureen's advice and set up a meeting with Sister Karen Marcil, who was at that time president of our order's Albany region. At our meeting, Sister Karen—who was familiar with my work and that of Farano House—knew I was stalling as I explained and restated the obvious. She asked me the exact purpose of this meeting.

I finally managed to get the sentence out. "I would like to be Barbara's foster mother," I said to my superior.

Presidential silence. Sister Karen needed some time to let it sink in. This was an unprecedented request, she said. It was her job to project into the future, and she had gathered from our conversations that I would seek to take the next step if Barbara became available for adoption. I had not hidden my deep desire to take care of Barbara as her mother, beginning with foster care and whatever else that might one day entail. I remember the president's words of caution: "This is very uncharted, very unknown territory for us. But once we head down this road, we all know there's no turning back."

Such a relationship—an active sister and at the same time an active mother—had never been allowed in the history of the Sisters of Mercy in this region. There seemed to be little or no precedent in religious life in general, either. Sister Karen said she had a lot to consider, and that, as president, she would discuss my request with the leadership team of the Sisters of Mercy's two-hundred-member Albany community. I couldn't hope for anything more. At least my proposal wasn't being dismissed out of hand, and it appeared to be taken seriously and given prompt attention.

It was hard to concentrate on my work as I waited to meet with Sister Karen two weeks later. The leadership team's response was not entirely encouraging. They weren't denying my request, but they felt it ran against the grain of the Sisters of Mercy's stated goals and philosophy. Sisters were many things: teachers, nurses, administrators, social workers, and more. But they weren't mothers. Not literally. Not legally.

Furthermore, the leadership team had many practical concerns that needed further exploration and evaluation. They raised a long list of difficult questions and legal issues. Was such a thing allowable under Roman Catholic canon law governing religious life? Would this break my vows of obedience, service, and even chastity? How could I continue to live in community with the other sisters given the demands of parenthood? Would I no longer be available to participate in Sisters of Mercy committees and projects? What would be the perception in the wider community, and would it damage the Sisters of Mercy's public image? Would it set a precedent, causing other sisters to expect they could do the same thing?

What would I do when Barbara got sick? Who would pay for the girl's health care and medical bills? What if Barbara's biological father also died, which was likely? Would I then automatically become the girl's adoptive mother and sole guardian? What if something happened to me and I could no longer provide adequate care for Barbara? What were the order's legal responsibility and liability in all this? Would there be a public backlash among conservative Catholic groups if word got out?

I felt demoralized by the leadership team's response but not entirely defeated. They raised some important issues I hadn't considered.

The next step for Sister Karen, who was planning ahead and anticipating the time in which I would seek adoption of Barbara, was to conduct a legal review. Two lawyers were consulted, a canon lawyer for the Albany Roman Catholic diocese and another who worked nationally. Neither found any legal grounds upon which to deny my request. There were a few cases around the country of sisters who filled in briefly as foster parents for children in crisis and in need of a temporary guardian. Permanent foster care among sisters was virtually unheard of and adoption unprecedented. And so I struggled to remain hopeful.

My optimism waned a bit more when I was contacted by Putnam County social-services officials, who said the delays concerned them. They informed me they would continue to search for other suitable foster parents for Barbara while the

Sisters of Mercy were reviewing my request. I took heart from the encouragement of the Farano House staff; they were rooting for me to get approval—and soon.

Sister Karen also wanted to consult with the bishop. Although the Sisters of Mercy were not technically under control of the bishop, the counsel of Bishop Howard Hubbard was significant. Bishop Hubbard was known as a progressive and empathetic leader. He had learned firsthand the pain and suffering of the poor and disenfranchised in the 1960s, when he was a street priest running Providence House, a storefront operation in one of Albany's inner-city neighborhoods, which gave hope to drug addicts and others in need of spiritual renewal and redemption.

I was pleased to have my request brought to the attention of Bishop Hubbard because I respected him enormously and knew he would be at once understanding and fair. I was encouraged by the fact that he had been very supportive of the work of Farano House since its founding. As bishop he had taken a special interest in assisting children with HIV and AIDS. After all, he had made time in his busy schedule to come to Barbara's birthday party. I had considered him a friend for many years, too, since he had volunteered his time as chaplain of Community Maternity Services and said Mass for clients and staff.

Bishop Hubbard began his response to my request to become Barbara's foster parent by recounting the life and work of Catherine McAuley, the Sisters of Mercy founder. She was considered a trailblazer, one who devoted herself to assisting the sick and poor in nineteenth-century Ireland, especially women and children. Mother McAuley's founding principle was to provide care for those shunned by society, and she was willing to reinterpret the rules of religious dogma and canon law to make that critical service possible. Bishop Hubbard suggested that if Mother McAuley had been alive in the 1980s when the AIDS epidemic struck America, she wouldn't have hesitated to provide care for women and their babies infected with the virus. He gave my request his endorsement. His support and historical perspective carried a lot of weight.

The bishop's opinion confirmed the findings of the canon lawyers, who could not locate any language in the canon law of the Roman Catholic Church that prevented a sister from being a temporary foster mother. It appeared as if my request had cleared the final hurdle. But there was one remaining obstacle. The leadership team called a final community-wide meeting to discuss my request.

I had talked about my desire to become Barbara's foster parent with several of my fellow sisters, but it probably wasn't widely known yet among our region's two hundred members. I was nervous as the community meeting got started. I had been rehearsing in my head my justification for this request and responses to the questions that I anticipated.

Only a handful of sisters attended, and their response at first was muted. I didn't know whether this favored my request or was a bad sign. I soon found out. Most who came voiced objections. One elderly sister was adamant that my request violated the vow of chastity. She argued that my being Barbara's foster mother would be an intimate, exclusive relationship. She felt very strongly that my request should be denied. Others in attendance were less specific and voiced vague reservations, but the underlying theme of their remarks was that for a Sister of Mercy to become a mother—even a temporary foster mother—crossed a line that they would not condone.

My first reaction was anger. They had gotten my Italian dander up. But this wasn't a forum where it would be appropriate for me to argue and fight back. My second thought was that I should have packed the meeting with my friends and supporters who could articulate my position forcefully and eloquently. I wanted Sister Maureen or one of my other close friends to describe how Barbara had lost her mother to the horrible disease of AIDS and how this little girl's strongest and deepest connection was now with me. I wanted someone to speak at the meeting about how I wanted to be the constant and nurturing presence in Barbara's life as she faced the challenges of living with the virus that leads to AIDS. My friends had offered to come to the meeting, but I hadn't anticipated such strong opposition and had told them their attendance wasn't necessary.

After the community meeting, I knew there would be a decision soon. What I didn't know was whether the opposition of a vocal minority would be enough to overturn the support of the bishop and the findings of the canon lawyers. I didn't have to wait long for an answer. The letter from Sister Karen as president of the Sisters of Mercy was formal and brief. But it was groundbreaking. My request was approved. I, Sister Mary Ann LoGiudice, could be a foster mother to Barbara.

Left:
Dressed in her Sunday best, baby Barbara takes some early steps.

Below:
Always a cut-up, Barbara, 5, laughs at her own joke as we share a funny moment during the Christmas season.

Left:
Barbara loves to dress up, and here she poses in an Easter outfit.

Below:
Beaming with a mother's joy, I hold my daughter, Barbara, 6, after our adoption ceremony in Family Court, flanked by the judge and court clerk. Barbara's best friend, Amanda, as always, is nearby.

Above:
This is one of my favorites among Barbara's drawings, in which she depicts a dream about being able to fly.

Center:
Barbara snuggles up, nestling in my arms.

Below:
"My special gift is life," Barbara says in her picture.

Such pure joy,
my daughter's beaming, sunny smile.

Right:
Barbara and Amanda in the surf at Cape Cod, our annual summer vacation destination.

Below:
Best friends forever, Amanda and Barbara, both 8, hug for a portrait on the front porch

Above:
I'm so proud of Barbara for making her
first communion. Joining in the liturgy
and celebration is our good friend, at left,
Father Tony Chiaramonte.

Facing page, above:
Barbara, 7, laughs during lunch at a beach
in Harwich on Cape Cod.

Facing page, below:
Her favorite Disney character, Goofy, wel-
comes Barbara at Disney World.

Barbara loves acting silly by dancing with an
inflatable Easter bunny at our home in Albany
a few months before her sixth birthday.

I share a precious moment with 3-year-old Barbara
amid the tulips at a park near Farano House
in Albany before she moved in with me.

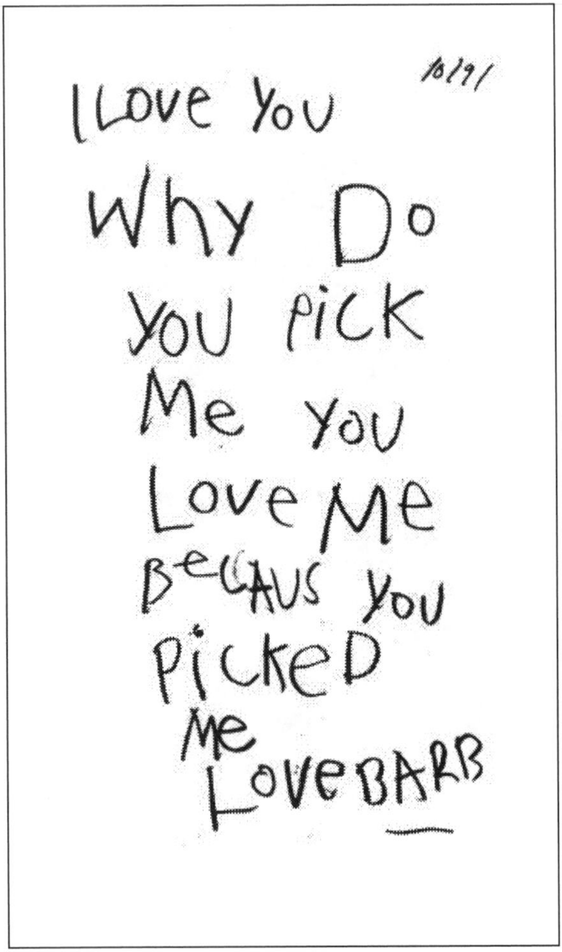

I LOVE YOU   10/9/

WhY Do
YOU PICK
Me YOU
Love Me
BECAUS YOU
PICKED
Me
LOVE BARB

Barbara expresses a daughter's love for her
adoptive mother, a letter I cherish.

Chapter Six

Making a New Home With Barbara

B arbara came to live with me just before Independence Day. It was an unorthodox arrangement, to say the least, even to friends. I was a Sister of Mercy, a single parent who had never raised a child before—although I had baby-sat nieces and nephews and coached teens through childbirth and the early stages of child rearing. Friends were happy for me and showed their support. Several relatives were initially wary, which I gathered from their response. The few acquaintances that knew about my becoming a foster parent were curious about this unique situation.

My reply to them all was the same. I said simply, "She loves me. I love her. Barbara has no one else to call Mother. We make each other whole."

That was the emotional part. The practical side was that this living arrangement required an adjustment for both of us. We lived in my three-bedroom, second-floor apartment on Kent Street, just six blocks from Farano House and my office.

A few friends and my sister Carmela, whom we call Mela, helped me paint and decorate Barbara's room. We stenciled a floral border on the wall, and I bought a white wicker bed, dresser, and chest set. I picked a Sesame Street theme for Barbara's sheets and towels.

When we had everything ready, I made a little ceremony of showing Barbara the space that would become a room of her own. I had her close her eyes and led her into the bedroom. She finally opened her eyes and looked around, silent and surprised.

"Who do you think this room is for?" I asked.

"It's for me!" Barbara said. She squealed for joy, jumped up and down, and bounded into my arms. I was overwhelmed with emotion and had to fight back tears.

Then Barbara said, "I'll be happy to come live with you. I'm a foster kid."

I couldn't speak. I was stunned and felt as if I had been kicked in the stomach. I set Barbara down on her bed without a word. She bounced on it a few times and scampered off, unaware of the hurt the term "foster kid" had caused me. I'd been very careful never to call Barbara *that*. Staff members at Farano House also avoided tagging children with that term, although Barbara must have picked it up from other kids there. To me it sounded as hard and mean as a curse. Foster kid. The new white wicker bedroom set seemed a little less shiny and bright at that moment. A pang of doubt rose in my throat, but I kept it to myself and said over and over in my head that everything was going to be fine.

I also did something I didn't often do on the spur of the moment. I said a little prayer asking for God's help. At dinner that night, Barbara began her ritual of leading us in grace before a meal. But she had her own special twist: singing grace to a bouncy beat. Of course she insisted that I, as well as any guests, sing along with enthusiasm.

Some of my close friends were former Sisters of Mercy. Among them was Marilyn Riley, part of a group that met for dinner at least once a month. Marilyn was special to Barbara for several reasons. Barbara loved to visit Marilyn because her mother, Marion Riley, lived with her. Marion told Barbara to call her Gram, and each time Barbara visited, Gram gave Barbara some money to buy a present for herself. Often, Gram proffered a twenty-dollar bill, and Barbara always stared at the cash in disbelief. Barbara liked to tell Amanda and her other friends, "Gram made me a rich girl."

Barbara also liked Marilyn's dog, a Lhasa apso named Clancy. Marilyn occasionally offered to watch Barbara overnight if I had to be out of town. Barbara, Marilyn, and little Clancy curled up together in the same bed and slept soundly—with a night light on at Barbara's request.

Barbara's probing nature always astounded Marilyn. Once, when Barbara was riding in her car, they noticed a rainbow on the horizon. Barbara started asking scientific questions about how rainbows were formed and about how they got their different colors—things Marilyn couldn't answer. Finally Marilyn broke into song, and Barbara, appeased, joined in on the chorus of "Somewhere Over the Rainbow."

Marilyn, who's single and does not have children, often told me how much joy Barbara brought into her life. When her mother died, Marilyn was especially touched by how Barbara tried to console her. "Don't be sad," the little girl told Marilyn. "Gram will be in heaven like my mommy is in heaven, and you'll be OK because I'm OK." Barbara had plenty of love and caring to spread around.

During this transition period, I was blessed with the joyous presence of family members. My brother Joe's five daughters, in particular, embraced Barbara as if she were their own little sister. None of them had children yet, and they were excited to be able to baby-sit her if I had to be away at a meeting or business function. My nieces spent a lot of time with us in our apartment and helped ease Barbara into her new living arrangement. My nieces assured me that Barbara was quickly becoming a natural extension of my life, that we even resembled each other somewhat in looks, and that we definitely shared certain attributes, a strong will—what some might construe as stubbornness—topping the list.

I was lucky to have wonderful neighbors, too. The tenants in the apartment below ours were college students, and Barbara enjoyed it when they played with her. The three young women went out of their way to spend a few minutes talking with Barbara when they passed and made plans for playing games together.

Barbara's favorite part of living on Kent Street was the second-floor screened porch. She loved to sit up there, pretending she was a princess who ruled all below. Thick green leaves from curbside trees enveloped our porch, and Barbara said she liked to imagine the porch was her own tree fort. We spent many happy hours on that porch, and given Barbara's enthusiasm and imagination, I also came to think of it as a real fort, our very own treetop retreat.

In Barbara's mind the location was ideal, since our apartment was just a short walk from McDonald's. We were well matched in that respect, too: I wasn't the greatest cook and Barbara wasn't the greatest eater, so we went to McDonald's often. Not that Barbara ate any better under the Golden Arches. She was a picky eater with a poor appetite and that never changed, no matter how many cheeseburgers, Chicken McNuggets, and french fries were placed before her. We did manage to amass a boxful of McDonald's Happy Meal toys, though, and that made the trips worthwhile to Barbara.

Mealtimes at the apartment proved to be a battle of wills. Stalling, she would push the food around on her plate, even though I tried to serve her favorites—macaroni and cheese, spaghetti, or some other pasta dish she claimed to enjoy. She knew how to manipulate me during our mealtime skirmishes, but I'd just dig in and become more rigid. Sometimes, though, I couldn't help but melt and relax the rules for this little girl. One night at dinner, Barbara promised she would eat better if she could have the plates her mommy in heaven had. "You just have to go to the blue house and look in a box under my bed. That's where we left them," Barbara said.

I tried to explain that the dishes—like the blue house, like her mommy, like their past together—were gone and couldn't be brought back except in her memory. We needed to build our own traditions and memories together, I said. It was our chance to begin anew. Barbara didn't fully understand my point, and I let it go.

This was the stage of development in which Barbara needed love and attention, not rules and rigidity. Given her situation, I became a lenient mother and made no apologies. I wasn't alone. My staff happily spoiled her, especially my administrative assistant, Kathleen O'Sullivan. Kathleen, a mother of two girls, took it upon herself to operate what amounted to an after-school program for Barbara. Each afternoon, Barbara would get picked up from school by Cathy Toedt, a CMS staff member, who brought her back to our offices at CMS for the few hours until I finished work.

Barbara had the run of the building and our other houses on the block, but she liked to spend most of her time with Kathleen. They'd play games like tic-tac-toe or hangman, draw pictures, and munch from a seemingly bottomless bag of popcorn. I'd pop my head in between meetings, or Barbara would scamper between Kathleen's office and mine if I was free. Barbara set the agenda. But she responded well to Kathleen's expertise in raising girls. Barbara did her homework for Kathleen with a minimum of fuss—something I struggled to get her to do. Kathleen had a large repertoire of inducements, such as ordering pizza for study breaks or promising Barbara that she could have a sleepover with Kathleen's daughters if she finished her homework assignments.

Most of all, Barbara liked to have Kathleen read her stories in the hours they shared together in Kathleen's office. Kathleen took the lead, but everyone on my staff was wonderful in making Barbara feel comfortable and at home in our office after school. I remember a red bike once came in as a donation to CMS, and the staff took turns pushing Queen

Barbara around my office. My staff also made special trips with Barbara across North Main Avenue to the pastoral center, where the bishop's office is located, for soda and snacks from the vending machines. I wasn't going to begrudge her a little spoiling, and I finally relented on the standoffs at mealtime over healthy eating habits. Barbara had always been a tiny child; she never weighed more than forty pounds. I vowed not to let my entreaties for her to eat become a source of stress. I still tried to get Barbara to eat more, but my muted requests were made only once or twice, and we didn't focus on them.

Barbara and I fell into a comfortable routine that I eventually realized was much like the patterns I knew as a child. I was my father's daughter, after all. Our Sundays were filled with family rituals that I'd put on hold in my first years as a sister. Now, as a mother, I relished bringing Barbara to church. We attended Mass at the Cathedral of the Immaculate Conception, a vastly ornate Gothic church in downtown Albany, and I didn't argue when she always chose the very first pew for us.

Barbara also sang in the children's choir with her best friend, Amanda, during religious education class. The two friends always stood shoulder to shoulder during the singing portion of Sunday school, heads leaning in toward each other, eyes staring at the sheet music, belting out the hymns with every fiber of their being. They didn't care what anyone else thought. From their mouths to God's ears. Their religious education teacher often told me she could have made an entire choir out of just Barbara's and Amanda's voices.

The two girls' joyous response to hymns and the liturgy

deeply touched me in a way I hadn't felt in church in years. Their enthusiastic and innocent faith rekindled my own devotion. By contrast, as a sister attending Mass solo, I'd quietly assume my place about three-quarters of the way back in the cathedral, a place at once anonymous and slightly less than fully committed. That wouldn't do with Barbara. She taught me so much, especially the simple act of putting myself literally out in front in whatever I did, including attending Mass. Rather than remaining inconspicuous, as was my custom, Barbara liked to wiggle her long, slender fingers from her front-row perch in a happy wave at the rector, Father Jones. He always returned Barbara's sly little greeting.

Though a child, Barbara possessed a profound spirituality. She may not have been conscious of it, but she pondered deep thoughts and often shared her search for meaning with me. She had a knack for surprising me with unfathomable queries when I was driving and fighting traffic. I remember when she was in the first or second grade, she asked me in the car, "Do kids grow up in heaven or do they stay young?" I almost drove off the road. I don't remember my response, but it was surely a vague muttering that in no way satisfied Barbara's intense questioning.

My salary as a Sister of Mercy was modest but adequate for a single woman. It didn't stretch enough to cover all of my additional expenses with Barbara, so I was grateful for a monthly foster-care subsidy check from Putnam County. Barbara, Amanda, and the other HIV-positive children from Farano House were classified as having special health needs and received about one thousand dollars each month, higher than the subsidies for healthy foster children. Barbara's medical bills were reimbursed by Medicaid as well. The financial piece of becoming Barbara's foster parent, about which some of the other sisters initially raised objections, never became an issue.

Of course, my spoiling of Barbara extended to her choice of wardrobe. She loved to dress in nice outfits, and her shorts and T-shirts always matched. Barbara's neatness came from her biological mother, I suspect, who always saw to it that her little girl's outfits were coordinated. Barbara also liked to wear frilly dresses for any occasion, and I indulged her fashion sense. Barbara fancied herself a little princess who preferred indoor games and activities. When she played outdoors, she was careful not to get dirty. She wanted her outfits to stay looking nice.

I remember our first summer together was a sweltering one. The forecast day after day was classic upstate New York: hazy, hot, and humid. I bought a small wading pool for our little backyard. But Barbara, the little princess, was tentative and would only go in the water if I did so first. Of course I always plopped right into the thing. I couldn't care less what the neighbors or friends who dropped by might think. This was our magical time together when the rest of the world was shut out. I loved the way Barbara's auburn hair—which I sometimes put in pigtails—bleached out in the summer and how the sun brought out her freckles. It made her look like the very picture of Pippi Longstocking. We splashed around together and pretended we were in the pool of a castle in our very own kingdom. Barbara always had a royal imagination.

"You be the mommy fish, and I'll be the baby fish," she said.

I loved hearing that, and I knew that it meant we had turned a corner in our adjustment to living together as mother and daughter. We played that fish game for a long time. Barbara called me "mommy fish" morning, noon, and night for two days.

On the third day of our wading pool play, Barbara called me simply "Mommy." I was stunned. I didn't say anything at first. I felt a lump rise in my throat and just let the word soak in. Finally, I told her that it sounded nice and I liked to be called Mommy. And that is what she called me from that moment on.

Barbara was four years old when we went on our first trip together, a summer vacation to Cape Cod with three of my friends—also Sisters of Mercy—and my sister Mela. It was our annual all-women trip that we'd been taking together for several summers. We looked forward to Cape Cod all year, but this summer was unique because Barbara was the first child to be brought along. Although we were all in agreement about letting her come, we knew our vacation would be different. Just how much different, we didn't imagine.

We had rented a home in Harwichport for two weeks, and it rained twelve of the fourteen days—mostly heavy downpours. Cape Cod in the rain is a special torment. The lovely beaches are viewed through the steady swipe of windshield wipers. We tried to counter the boredom with rainy-day activities for Barbara. We read books. Sang along to tapes of children's songs. Played games like tic-tac-toe, Old Maid, and Candy Land. We were exhausted by late morning. Luckily, we had brought a truckload of videotapes, and Barbara watched *The Little Mermaid* and other movies over and over again. It kept raining. I couldn't get Barbara to nap. The afternoons and evenings dragged on.

Being stuck in the house in the rain did not bring out the best in Barbara. She was demanding and cranky much of the time. To be honest, so was I. We were doing the early steps of the mother-daughter dance, sizing each other up, and it wasn't pretty to be exploring that challenging terrain in the rain on Cape Cod. Barbara already had learned how to push my buttons, of course, and she played my frayed emotions like a maestro handles a grand piano. Friction filled the rental house as the rain continued to drum on the roof. The group seemed connected only by its shared frustration. This is what we'd looked forward to all year?

The rain continued to fall. One afternoon, I lost it and started to yell at Barbara. She was in the throes of another tantrum, and I couldn't take it anymore. I announced to anyone who would listen that I had had it and left the house, got into my car, and drove to the nearest phone booth. Sobbing, I called my friend Tony, the priest. "What was I thinking, Tony?" I asked between sobs. "I can't do this. I can't do this."

Chapter Seven

Raising a Daughter

The rain finally broke, at least figuratively, and the Cape Cod vacation eventually became a running joke among all of us. Even Barbara liked to laugh about it. Our first summer drew to a close and, in retrospect, seemed too short. I'd received a crash course on being a working mother, and most evenings I was just plain exhausted from the demands of raising Barbara, running a large social-services agency, and staying active in commitments to my religious community. Fall was approaching, and I hadn't yet signed up Barbara for a day-care center.

I didn't bargain on the education I got when I went in search of a day-care program for Barbara, now four years old. I was torn over how to treat her HIV status. Some of my colleagues counseled me to keep it confidential during the interviews, but my style has always been straightforward and upfront. It's how I was raised and it's how I would proceed in this matter. My naiveté was quickly exposed, however.

I took Barbara to visit a highly recommended day-care center. She busied herself with toys in a play area as I sat down with the director. I immediately informed him that Barbara had tested positive for HIV. The director stared blankly at me, and there was a long silence before he stammered a response. He said it would not be appropriate to accept Barbara with so much fear and uncertainty surrounding the virus. He had the other children and their parents to think about. I tried to explain my side of things, but he cut me off.

"Besides," the director said, "we're here to prepare young children for school. With that disease, she might not even make it to school."

Barbara had come into the director's office at this point, but it wasn't clear if she'd heard the remark. My face flushed crimson, and my hands clenched into fists as I bit my lip to contain my anger. It took a lot of restraint not to fire something back at the director, choice expletives he probably wouldn't expect from a sister. Instead I took Barbara by the hand and, without saying a word, marched out of the center. I never returned, although I did write a scathing letter to the director, letting him know exactly what I thought of his tactless remarks with Barbara in the room—and his ignorance about HIV.

I didn't let that first encounter dissuade me, but that response became a disturbing pattern as I visited three more day-care centers in the Albany area. I told each of them up front that Barbara had HIV, and all three apologized but said they could not find room for her. I'd never experienced such blatant rejection. I felt the sting of discrimination for the first time in my life and learned a powerful lesson about prejudice.

Barbara didn't share my outrage. She didn't want to go to day care anyway. She wanted to stay at Farano House while I worked. It was what she knew, and she was happy, safe, and comfortable there. Since my office was right across the street, I could visit her throughout the day. Her best friend, Amanda, was at Farano, and they never grew tired of playing together, making up games, or just talking. But Farano House was not a day-care center. Rather, it was a temporary residence for infants and preschoolers needing care. What was I going to do with Barbara come September?

Times like these made me wonder whether I was cut out to be a mother after all. It wasn't that I lacked the background and experience for the job, although I needed to remind myself of my qualifications from time to time. For starters, I helped teach teen mothers the basics of parenting. I was also a regular baby-sitter for a platoon of nieces and nephews. But all that was essentially shift work. My relatives came to pick up their kids after a few hours, or at most a few days, and I was left with time and space to do what I wanted to do. I experienced the joys, albeit short-lived, without the full-time parenting responsibilities.

Nothing I had done before prepared me for the totality of being a mother. It was now and tomorrow and forever. And everything in between. The teen mothers in my program were fond of calling it "24/7"—for all the hours in a day and all the days in a week. I always considered that slang a bit of hyperbole—that is, until Barbara became my daughter and I learned firsthand how accurate the 24/7 shorthand truly is.

Before I became Barbara's foster mother, I liked to think of myself as a relatively giving person. Religious life trained me for a ministry of selflessness and service to others. That was the theory, at least. What I quickly learned was that there was no service as all-encompassing as that of being a mother. By taking care of Barbara, I developed a new respect for the single teen mothers in my program. After all, I was struggling as a forty-something single mother myself, even though I had a broad network of family and friends for support and no serious financial worries. Many of the teen mothers, on the other hand, had to go it alone with almost no backup. Barbara helped me see the world differently and raised both my level of awareness and my empathy for people who are struggling and suffering.

Being a mother brought about other lifestyle adjustments for which I wasn't prepared. Although my best friends remained close and supported my bringing Barbara into our friendship, a few of my acquaintances who didn't care to make time for Barbara drifted away. Helen Hayes, a former Sister of Mercy I first met at the convent, was one of my long-time friends who didn't warm right away to my new routine. She made no secret of her initial opposition to my decision. Helen didn't think I had thought through completely how taking care of a young child would change everything irrevocably—our friendship included. In the long run, though, our friendship endured, and Barbara became a regular visitor to Helen's house and Helen's parents' house.

The short-term reality was that I no longer had time for the kind of socializing I had previously enjoyed with Helen and a close-knit circle of friends. Before, we had all liked going out to the movies together or to late dinners in fine restaurants, and I could accept spur-of-the-moment invitations. Now I had to say no because of Barbara. I couldn't get a baby-sitter on such short notice, and I didn't want to leave her too often in the evening anyway.

Thankfully, a new extended family gradually began to form around Barbara and me. It was made up of my relatives and friends who were glad to incorporate Barbara into new routines and new activities. They were the friends, I decided, who were willing to ride out this challenging transition period with me.

One of them was Mary Jo Slowey, whom I first met as a volunteer at CMS in 1982. She was placed with my agency through the Jesuit Volunteer Corps after graduating from college with a social-work degree. Mary Jo was so good as a volunteer that I hired her as a paid staff member, and she stayed on at CMS for another two years before moving to a new position in Baltimore. Despite a decade separating us in age and the geographical distance between us, Mary Jo and I have remained good friends.

I liked combining trips to see my sister Connie in Maryland and to visit Mary Jo. Mary Jo also occasionally joined Barbara and me on vacation and came to stay with us for a few days in Albany each summer. I'll always remember how Mary Jo helped Barbara construct her own water-slide world: a tarp, a hose, and an inflatable pool at the bottom of a hill. Barbara loved to slip and slide with Mary Jo. Mary Jo's visits were a touchstone for both Barbara and me, and her friendship brightened our lives.

Barbara's network of friends at Farano House and along

North Main grew stronger and larger all the time. Barbara was especially close to Sister Helen, who had come from Ireland and worked as a staff member and cook at Farano House. I'd pick up Sister Helen in my car, since she didn't own one, and we'd drive to work together in the morning— she, Barbara, and I singing kiddie songs all the way. She had a lovely lilting brogue that captivated Barbara. Sister Helen also liked to take Barbara and Amanda on special outings, including a trip to K-mart to have the girls' portrait done together. For their photo background they chose the message, "Thank Heaven for Little Girls." After the photo session, Sister Helen later told me, Barbara grew introspective and said to her, "My mommy Angeline is in heaven, and she asked God to send me a special person, and that's how Mary Ann came to be my mommy."

It wasn't long before friends were noticing that Barbara was taking after me. She wanted her hair cut in a short bob like mine, and she picked up a lot of my expressions. I have a way of rolling my eyes when I'm bored, and Barbara was soon doing the same thing. One expression I instilled in her, which I'm not wild about, is my way of declaring my exasperation: "I'm sick of it." That turned a few heads coming from the mouth of a five-year-old girl. I'd smile weakly with a "that's-my-daughter" look. Another trick of hers when we were in a nice restaurant always invited the stares of other diners: she would knock back containers of half-and-half as if they were shots of whiskey. I'd grin sheepishly as she slurped down each coffee creamer. What could I say? "Yep, that's my girl."

Barbara fancied herself the queen of North Main Avenue

and made it a point to know and visit everybody up and down the block. There was our good friend Father Tony, for instance. His counseling office was just a few houses away, and it was a sanctuary for Barbara when she was looking for a diversion from her daily routine. Given her difficult early childhood, I thought it was important that she have some positive male role models in her life. She was indeed blessed with numerous good men who took an active and nurturing interest in her development. She became very close to Father Tony and had no qualms about arriving at his office unannounced and informing his secretary to break into a counseling session. "I know he would want to see me and talk to me," Barbara would tell her.

Barbara summed up her bond with Father Tony, whom she called simply Tony, in a letter she wrote to him in third grade. He has it framed and hanging on his office wall next to a picture of the two of them. The letter says, "Tony is a really funny guy. He takes me places. He tucks me in bed. He makes me laugh. He even tickles me. He shaved off his mustache. He's the greatest friend a girl could ever have. Barbara."

Barbara established a different but equally important relationship with Father Chris, who is the head of campus ministry at the College of Saint Rose, just around the corner from Farano House. I'd known Chris since the early 1970s, when he was a seminarian assigned to St. Patrick's Church in Albany one summer and I was a social-outreach worker there. I made good use of Chris' abilities as a handyman. He was Mr. Fix-It around my house, someone I always leaned on to mend Barbara's broken toys, to help us put up our

Christmas tree, and to make general household repairs. He even fixed my car on occasion.

Chris taught Barbara to ice-skate at Swinburne Park near our house. He introduced her to astronomy and shared his knowledge of the night sky. Barbara learned to point out constellations and impressed me with the information she picked up from Chris about Mars, Venus, and other planetary matters. This in turn led to discussions about heaven and spirituality. Chris always called Barbara an adult in a little body, and he engaged her on that level.

I once bought a package of glow-in-the-dark stick-on stars for Barbara's bedroom ceiling. They sat in the package until Chris came over one night and Barbara asked him to put them up. He did and they glowed like a celestial vision above her bed. Barbara devised her own planetarium and liked to invite visitors into her room, one at a time, particularly my sister friends. She instructed them to lie on her bed, close their eyes, be quiet, and face heavenward. Then she flicked off the light switch and told them to open their eyes. Constellations glowed ethereally in the inky darkness of her bedroom. Of course, being the entrepreneur she was, Barbara charged each viewer a quarter per session. They paid. When I found out about her moneymaking scheme, I told Barbara I was proud of her enterprising ways, but I thought the proceeds should be sent to the needy. She argued a bit but saw my point.

Above all, Chris brought to my experience with Barbara a profoundly insightful and unsentimental view of our relationship. To those who wanted to make me out as some sort of big-hearted sister who did a noble thing in taking care of this unfortunate orphaned child with HIV, Chris said, "Bunk." Barbara was the teacher, not the other way around. We learned from her. Chris reminded those romantic sorts, and me occasionally, that we all were the beneficiaries of a remarkable girl who came unexpectedly into our world and had a lot to teach adults—especially priests and sisters in religious life—about embracing the moment and facing difficulties and disease with a joyous spirit. On a subconscious level, Chris said Barbara changed his understanding of what life and death are all about, and she helped teach him to trust in the mystery of that journey.

In addition to our priest friends who filled Barbara's need for strong male role models, there was my brother Joe, my brother-in-law Art, a couple of nephews, and Al Turo. Al was a diocesan executive and a Farano volunteer. He met Barbara at a block party celebrating the twentieth anniversary of CMS. Barbara liked to stop by his office across the street in the pastoral center to chat, draw pictures, eat chips, drink soda, and munch candy that she purchased in a vending machine with Al's never-ending supply of coins. The two of them liked to walk to Ben & Jerry's for ice cream and to kick a soccer ball. Barbara loved to play soccer, and I tried to join in, but she wasn't thrilled with my lack of ability and sought out better athletes when she could. Al always made time for Barbara, even when work and family commitments packed his schedule, and she enjoyed their time together—especially playing soccer.

As a mother I cherished new rituals that involved just Barbara and me. There was our evening bath, games, maybe a video. I would read Barbara bedtime stories. She couldn't get enough of a picture-book collection called *Free to Be ... You and Me*. I think we wore out the poem titled "Don't Dress Your Cat in an Apron." Barbara could recite it at warp speed: "Don't dress your cat in an apron just 'cause he's learning to bake. Don't put your horse in a nightgown just 'cause he can't stay awake. Don't dress your snake in a muumuu just 'cause he's off on a cruise. Don't dress your whale in galoshes if she really prefers overshoes. A person should wear what he wants to and not just what other folks say. A person should do what she likes to. A person's a person that way."

No matter how many stories I read to her, though, Barbara managed to fight me about going to sleep. It was another battle of wills along the lines of our dinnertime conflicts. I tried everything I knew to get her to go to bed, and she would argue with me and simply refuse. One night my frustration boiled over at that point and I yelled at her, which reduced her to tears. Finally, when she had stopped sobbing, she told me why she was crying.

"When my mommy in heaven died, they told me she went to sleep," Barbara said. "I'm afraid if I go to sleep, I'll die too."

I reached over and lifted Barbara's frightened little body into my arms and carried her into my bedroom in the front of the apartment. I had a queen-sized bed, and I tucked her under the covers and got in beside her. I held this little girl, my daughter, who was as tiny and light as a bird. I rubbed her thin back, stroked her hair, and caressed her soft cheeks.

But something was terribly wrong. Night after night I cried until my eyes were red and my head ached. Barbara needed so much care and at times demanded more than I could provide by myself. I worried that I didn't have enough to give her. I prayed, but prayers had lost their redemptive power for me. Prayers and daily meditations had brought answers and comfort for my concerns as a sister but seemed unable to provide me with the strength and guidance I sought as a mother. As I grew more tired, my prayer sessions became shorter and more irregular.

Despite my lack of attentiveness to prayer, Barbara had ways of challenging my faith, and her child's questioning helped me confront some spiritual issues. I remember when she asked me, "Mommy, what does a spirit look like?"

Well, that's one they didn't test us on in the convent. So I stalled and finally offered up a rather pathetic definition of a spirit being like an invisible poof or swirl of air, but we know it's there. That made Barbara question me more. She asked, "How will I recognize my mommy in heaven if she's just a poof of air?" More silence. Finally I muttered, "Don't worry. Your mommy will find you."

Some weeks I don't know if I consciously tried to pray at all. I went to bed earlier, too, and slid noiselessly into my bed beside Barbara. As with mealtimes, I had given in on the battle over bedtime. I didn't force Barbara to stay in her own bed if she was scared or just having a difficult time sleeping. Some might have criticized my lenient parenting, but at the end of a long day I felt too tired from a single mother's work to try to maintain textbook discipline.

Another new experience for me was joining a support group. I hadn't been very comfortable with the concept before, but suddenly I found myself reaching out, hungry for knowledge about being a parent of a child with HIV. I located a support group for parents of such children. I was reluctant and skeptical at first about joining in the discussions fully and openly, but soon I became comfortable with the other parents and found them very helpful and wonderfully giving people. I took away a lot from this sharing of ideas, laughter, and tears.

Barbara and I established an important annual mother-daughter ritual during our second year living together. She began to join me each October at the end of an eight-day spiritual retreat for seven Sisters of Mercy at the Benedictine priory in Weston, Vermont. Barbara was the first child invited to come to the priory during our retreat—I was unique among the sisters in having a daughter, after all—and her presence was a memorable experience that enriched our lives, and hers, in many ways.

The Weston Priory is located in central Vermont, about thirty miles from Manchester, in the foothills of the Green Mountains. The hillsides are ablaze with fiery fall foliage during the first week of October, when I've made the retreat with six other Sisters of Mercy since 1985. The priory grounds are breathtaking at that time of year. We stay in a house named Bethany, a nineteenth-century farmhouse the brothers restored when they founded the priory in the early 1960s. Bethany is as resonant as its name, with exposed beams, a large stone fireplace, wide-plank pine floors, a huge kitchen, and a large picture window in the living room with a panoramic view of the surrounding mountains and the pristine ponds dotting the property.

There's no more inviting place to feel like a community of sisters than at Bethany, working together after a day of individual prayer and meditation to prepare a dinner shared at a big dining room table and talking late into the night around a roaring fire. We all considered those eight days each October a kind of *sanctum sanctorum*, a powerful force for individual spiritual renewal and communal unity. Into this circle of sisterhood, Barbara was welcomed as a special visitor.

The idea of having my daughter come to the Weston Priory on the final weekend of our retreat grew out of a mother's guilt. The first year Barbara was living with me, she stayed with my family during my retreat. Before I left, I had wrapped and laid out eight presents—one for each day I was gone—and called her before she went to bed each night. She wouldn't say much on those nightly calls, other than to repeat that she wasn't pleased I was not at home with her. The second year, I came up with the plan of having a friend drive Barbara to Weston for the end of the retreat, which was always Columbus Day weekend. The other sisters empathized with my situation, and after some discussion with the brothers, it was agreed that Barbara could join us.

The dozen Benedictine brothers, who live in a cloistered community, invite the public to daily prayer and Masses on a regular basis, and they also make their grounds and houses available for retreats. They support themselves by cultivating crops, making and selling pottery, and running a religious bookstore. In addition to the spectacularly beautiful scenery, the priory offers an ambience of prayerful solitude and contemplative peacefulness. It is the most meaningful sanctuary and profoundly spiritual setting I've ever found in my travels. For Barbara it was an opportunity to spend time with her mother in an atmosphere of authentic religious life and spiritual community. In other words, to allow her to see me at my most sisterly, if you will. Neither of us was quite sure what to expect of this experiment.

Sister Jane Silk, a Sister of Mercy in Georgetown, Connecticut, who is well known for her retreat work, has been our retreat director since we started at Weston Priory in 1985. Sister Jane helped us to reflect upon our lives individually and as a community and to renew our commitment to a prayer life that encompasses every aspect of our everyday work and routine. She reminded us that prayer should not be something reserved for church or limited to Sundays. Our retreat work deepened my faith and helped me feel closer to God. In a way, Barbara as a child of God also enhanced those same areas of my spiritual development.

The year I first brought Barbara to the retreat, Sister Jane and her housemate, Sister Jeanne Snyder, brought their new puppy, a black pointer mix named Jigs. Barbara and Jigs were a match made in heaven. They romped and played and entertained each other. The puppy tired out first. Jigs snoozed. That's when Barbara, who was used to being the only child in an adult world and possessed poise beyond her years, really took center stage. She assumed a place at the head of the dining room table and led the dinner time conversation, a pint-sized raconteur. This surprised no one other than our retreat director. The other sisters were among a group who got together once a month or so in Albany for dinner, and Barbara had been a frequent guest at those gatherings.

But the Weston experience was a heightened moment. We were nine religious women, ten counting Barbara, sharing and living as a community. My close friend, Sister Jane McCullough, the director of postulants at the convent when I entered, was an original member of the retreat group and a favorite audience member for Barbara. Sister Jane considered Barbara part stand-up comic and part teacher of sisters. Sister Jane told me she learned from Barbara's addition to our retreat group not only how to laugh from her very soul but how to reclaim the silly joy of childhood. Barbara had invited Sister Jane to her birthday party for her mommy in heaven, after all, so she was somebody special. Sister Jane was also nice enough to make room for Barbara in the bedroom we shared in Bethany House and moved to the sofa downstairs, leaving her bed for Barbara. But mice skittered in the attic many nights and frightened Barbara so terribly that the only way to get her to sleep was to push the two single beds together and let her sleep next to me.

When we gathered at night around a roaring fire, Barbara took on the role of teacher for a group of sisters who had decades of classroom experience to their credit. Barbara taught us all how to sing silly nonsense ditties and told us knock-knock jokes and goofy stories that made us laugh until our sides hurt and the tears came. Barbara had a captive audience and she knew it. She strutted her stuff upon the Weston Priory stage, and each year the sisters wanted her back for a repeat performance.

Barbara wasn't all giggles and goofiness, though. She was deeply touched by the quiet power of the Benedictine brothers. She'd come with me to early morning prayer or Mass in the lovely stone chapel. The brothers made Barbara feel special and welcome. They also introduced her to a

Guatemalan family for whom the brothers had provided sanctuary from political and religious persecution. This couple and their children sang Guatemalan folk songs and told stories about their homeland. Barbara liked to spend time with them, and throughout the year, she would send pictures and letters to them and to the brothers, receiving cards from them in return. It was a meaningful new connection, and Barbara looked forward to renewing that friendship each October.

Best of all, the retreat was a chance for Barbara and me to spend long hours of solitude together during the closing weekend. We walked the nearby trails and took short drives into the picture-postcard-perfect Vermont villages. Barbara loved to study the ponds, waiting to see fish and frogs. But the most memorable discovery she made was the fluttering of yellow butterflies above the ponds of Weston. She found them to be fascinating creatures, so beautiful and delicate, yet capable of remarkable flights of endurance. She drew pictures of yellow butterflies over and over after that. They became a kind of emotional touchstone for her, deepening her interest in anything that had to do with winged insects.

The Weston retreat was a time of serenity, togetherness, and mutual growth for both of us. I cherished every moment with my daughter at the priory. It made me a better sister and a better mother. And in a small way, I think, it allowed the other sisters to experience the joys and challenges of parenting along with me.

Finally, back on the education front, just before school started that fall of 1988, I managed to secure a day-care opening at St. Mary's School in East Greenbush. It helped that I had a connection. The principal, Sister Penny Lynch, was a Sister of Mercy and a friend who often joined the Cape Cod group. As principal, Sister Penny was concerned about the other parents' fears over HIV. After discussing it, we decided that confidentiality was necessary, and Barbara's HIV status was disclosed only to the principal and her teachers. The same arrangement was made for Amanda. The two best friends split a full-time slot at St. Mary's. Barbara went two days a week and Amanda three. The girls spent the rest of their time together at Farano House.

My staff and I had come up with a creative solution to our day-care dilemma. I thought it was an ideal solution, but my experience taught me to be cautiously optimistic. From the start, Barbara was happy at St. Mary's and told me all about her day and the many things she liked to do and the friends she had made.

Fall flew by and soon the holidays were approaching. For Christmas Barbara's class put on a school play about the Nativity, and she was given the part of an angel. She was so proud of that. She told me that her mommy in heaven's name sounded like "angel"—Angeline. Barbara loved to draw pictures of angels, and she said that she dreamed her pictures could lift off the sheet of paper and fly, happy and free. Barbara also never forgot when one of my nieces told her, "Every time a bell rings, an angel gets its wings." Barbara delighted at hearing the bell ring several times each day at school, and the sound always made her think of angels.

Getting into a routine and making new friends at St. Mary's had been a godsend. It seemed, too, that the confidence she acquired there helped Barbara outgrow her nightmares of dying in her sleep.

I told myself I didn't have the time to get involved in the parents' group at St. Mary's. Part of it was my concern about other parents asking too many questions about Barbara and me. We needed to keep Barbara's HIV secret, and trying to make small talk while protecting that confidentiality seemed awkward. The other piece is that I felt like an outsider, somehow different. When I picked up Barbara after school each day, I felt set apart from the other mothers. I didn't wear a habit and veil or carry a rosary, but they knew I was a sister and their Catholic upbringing kicked in. They addressed me formally, as Sister Mary Ann. I wanted to ask them to call me just Mary Ann. But I never did and found excuses to slip away with a minimum of contact with other parents.

The spring of 1989 arrived full of promise. After a long winter indoors—Barbara was so thin she always felt cold and I wasn't much interested in winter sports—the two of us felt bright and warm and renewed again. Barbara was having a lot of fun with Amanda and her new friends at St. Mary's. She was healthy and radiated happiness. For the first time, the match felt just right, as it was meant to be, and the reality of our lives met my expectations when I'd first contemplated adoption.

I also received my first Mother's Day card that spring. Barbara had drawn flowers and in big block letters had written, "Mommy. I love you. Barbara." The card came with a paper cup sprouting with marigolds. Barbara had planted the flowers as seeds, had watered and cared for them, and now proudly presented them to me. I was awestruck. It was suddenly so real and beautiful. I kept saying to myself, "My

God, I'm this sweet little girl's mother." It felt so right.

We celebrated by going to McDonald's. Barbara didn't eat, of course, but that was OK. We brought the marigolds back to our Kent Street apartment and planted them in our little backyard. The yellow flowers blossomed. Summer came and we splashed once more in the wading pool. Mommy fish and baby fish, together forever.

Chapter Eight

The Bond of Best Friends

Barbara and Amanda had become best friends soon after they met at Farano House in the spring of 1988. Both were three years old at the time. That's where the similarities ended.

Barbara was a jabberer and prone to being bossy. Even as a preschooler, she was very opinionated and loved to debate—some might call it argue. At any rate, she could rationalize her arguments, support her positions, and always had to have the last word. (Maybe the LoGiudice genes were rubbing off on her, after all.) All of Farano House was a stage to her and she strutted upon it, learning how to perform in order to get her way. Barbara especially knew how to put things over on Amanda, being the consummate persuader she was.

Adults also fell under her spell. She was a charmer, and she knew it. As time went on Barbara became the elder stateswoman of Farano, and she discovered how to milk that role—especially when she argued (debated) over having to take naps along with the younger children.

Amanda, on the other hand, practically defined the term "laid back." She was quiet and submissive, with a sweetness that was like soft jazz played as background music. Despite their differences, Barbara and Amanda each quickly learned to accommodate the other's personality, and they essentially became a matched set. Two sides of the same coin. Barbara led, Amanda followed, and each got what she needed out of that dynamic. To see them skipping and singing as they approached a shopping mall, eagerly awaiting a clothing purchase, was to see two girls in love with life. Of course Barbara took the high road there, too, and insisted as they vamped through the clothing aisles that Amanda address her alternately as "darlink" and "Queen Barbara." After a brief rolling of her eyes, Amanda always went along with the routine—the demure sidekick to Barbara's stand-up comedy act.

Another thing that bound them together was their shared "apartness." They knew they were different from other kids they had both come to Farano as orphans. There was that "foster kid" tag they picked up, but both resolved in their own minds to make the best of a new home and situation. Those challenges drew them closer in the long run. It would be several years before they were told they had HIV. The virus then became a secret they shared and talked about together, but only with each other. That was a sacred trust neither violated.

Our friend Father Tony saw the girls often and liked to join Barbara, Amanda, and me for dinner on a regular basis. His favorite annual duty was to take Barbara and Amanda trick-or-treating around the neighborhood on Halloween. The two best friends made Tony laugh like nobody else could.

Tony came to think of Amanda and Barbara as keys on a piano. Ebony and ivory. Tony taught them the Paul McCartney and Stevie Wonder song by that name. Amanda and Barbara, black and white, struck perfect chords together. Most of the time.

They had their moments, of course. The staff at Farano told me about one particular day in which the two argued all day and carried on because Amanda was allowed to go without socks and Barbara wasn't. They always wanted to do the same thing. Even-steven. Maybe that explains how they came to prefer wearing identical outfits, especially Halloween costumes. They both sucked their thumbs in mirror images when they watched videos or listened to storybooks before bed.

They parted company, however, when it came to food. Amanda was a good eater and ate almost anything when she first arrived at Farano. But Barbara's finicky palate soon rubbed off on her best friend, and Amanda started turning up her nose at some of the meals she had previously enjoyed just because Barbara didn't like them. Barbara encouraged Amanda to try one of her favorite bath-time routines: playing in the tub while a staff member supplied her with a steady stream of Lifesaver candy. Quite the queen, she was.

And did I mention the Barbie dolls? Barbara and Amanda had a vast collection. I often felt that our house had been taken over by the preternaturally perfect doll. It was a Barbie universe. I just happened to live in it.

The two best friends could bicker with gusto. That's when I was reminded they were regular kids and all was fine. Around my circle of friends in Catholic Charities and the Sisters of Mercy, Barbara and Amanda were known alternately as "the little ladies" and "the girls" and "the best friends." On those occasions when they launched into side-by-side full-throttle tantrums, they earned the tag "the little beasties." When they argued or had a falling-out over some presumed transgression on Amanda's part, Barbara would say, "I'm not going to be your friend anymore and you can't come to my birthday party." But Amanda had the perfect comeback: "You already invited me." Usually, before their run-ins got to this level of friendship fracture, they would repair the damage by both blurting out the word "eyeball." It cracked them up every time. It was some sort of giggle-trigger or deep inside joke I didn't try to decipher.

From their earliest friendship, Barbara, more than Amanda, was aware of racial divisiveness. Barbara was a little spitfire in a pageboy haircut who challenged kids she didn't know with this warning: "Amanda is black, and she's my best friend, and if anybody does anything to her, I'll punch them out." It was this sort of pronouncement that earned Barbara the nickname among my family of Miss Babs.

Whenever they could, the two girls laughed and played together most of their waking hours. Barbara was the quick-witted ringleader who engineered the mischief. She was a pip in every sense of the word. I remember riding in our friend June's car, with Amanda and Barbara in the backseat. Guess who offered a running commentary? If June took too long at an intersection when the light changed, Barbara piped up with this gem: "It's not going to get any greener." Barbara never met my father, but it's the kind of line I can hear him saying.

Another time, when she saw my brother Joe eradicating some pesky bugs at his house, Barbara blurted out, "Joe, you wouldn't be killing those ants if you saw *Honey, I Shrunk the Kids.*" She could get away with such chutzpah with my brother Joe, who, along with his wife, Mary, served as surrogate grandparents to Barbara and showered her with a deluge of unconditional love. They had fallen under the little girl's spell, and they were always there for Miss Babs, as Joe called her, whether it was attending a school function or having her over to their house to play. Mary tried encouraging Barbara to help in her vegetable garden in the summer, but she told Mary in no uncertain terms that she had no intention of digging weeds and getting dirt under her fingernails—a notion unbecoming a little princess. Barbara had her pierced earrings and black patent leather shoes to think of, don't you know.

Joe and Barbara became buddies. She liked the way he sang tunes to her, such as "Barbara Ann" and "I've Been Working on the Railroad" and "Rock My Soul in the Bosom of Abraham." Years later, she informed Joe with utmost seriousness that she now knew what a bosom was and that he should stop singing that song. She liked to be quizzed by Joe on trivia, such as which state has the most states bordering it (Kentucky) and the names of all the planets in our solar system. When Joe set up a croquet set in their living room, with his wife Mary's approval, there was no better rainy-day activity in Barbara and Amanda's book.

Joe had a way of making even the most mundane things

fun—even trips to the hospital, when he got the two best friends going on the game of scouting license plates. Both were thrilled the day they found an Iowa license plate in the hospital parking lot. Miss Babs and Joe were very special pals, and his friendship extended to Amanda. He and Barbara could get Amanda to laugh like nobody's business.

But one thing in Amanda's life made her sad: that Barbara had a mommy and Amanda did not. Amanda started asking how she could get a mommy. It was the one thing about Barbara's life that made Amanda jealous. Amanda talked a lot about how much she wanted a mommy. She eventually got her wish. Amanda was adopted by June Carlson, who had worked as a volunteer at Farano. The kids loved June, especially Amanda. Barbara gave her the nickname June Bug.

June was in her mid-thirties at the time and lived with her mother, Stella Carlson. June was quiet and easygoing, much like Amanda, and they made a good match. Beginning with their trial weekend together, Amanda and June seemed meant for each other. Theirs was an unlikely alliance. June had two older sisters, but there was a large age gap, and she grew up essentially as an only child. She earned a college degree in the humanities and seemed satisfied with an office job at a realtors' trade association. June and her mother, Stella, who had a clerical job in state government, enjoyed a quiet life.

June's life was altered forever when she was diagnosed with diabetes. She had lost her right leg at the knee before Amanda came into her life, and she wore a prosthesis. She walked with a slight limp and drove a car with her good foot, the left, but very few people knew about the extent of her diabetes or that she wore an artificial limb. Much later June told Amanda, "You don't have to tell people you have AIDS, and I don't have to tell people I have diabetes." I think part of the connection between June and Amanda was a shared understanding of living with illness.

June's mother, Stella, is a wonderfully open person, who welcomed Amanda into her life when she was in her late seventies. Both Amanda and Barbara loved Stella and called her "Granny." Barbara once remarked, loud enough for Stella to hear, "Granny's old, but she still can cook good." Barbara also expressed her amazement that Granny could open a car door with her old, wrinkly hands. Granny, Barbara, and Amanda made quite a trio on their outings.

June, Stella, and Amanda weren't everyone's idea of a textbook family unit. Stella told me that June occasionally was stopped by a passerby or a coworker who would raise the race issue. "Doesn't it bother you that she's black?" one woman bluntly asked, with Amanda just out of earshot. Meek, softspoken June bristled at that and was firm and angry in her response: "I never think about what color she is. She's my daughter and I love her." Privately, with her mother, June sometimes joked that she was the minority in the relationship and referred to herself at those times as "the diabetic amputee." June's and Amanda's admiration for each other was mutual. Amanda didn't think of June as disabled and saw beyond her physical ailments.

I remember when Barbara came home to me after her first sleep-over at Amanda's house with June and Stella. She was breathless with this revelation: "Mommy, there's something about June I don't think you know. June's leg comes off!" I thanked her for sharing that news with me and acted as if it were the most natural thing in the world. And that was that. In a child's resilient and accepting nature, Barbara never saw a need to discuss June's prosthesis again.

Barbara did like to talk a lot about Stella's grandson, Craig. He came to live with June and Stella when he was attending a local college. Amanda and Barbara thrived on the attention Craig gave them. Craig also served as a positive male role model for Amanda, who did not have any contact with her biological father. Unlikely as it might have appeared to outsiders, this three-generation, multicultural grouping—Stella, June, Craig, and Amanda—was transformed into a loving and supportive family through the power of acceptance and a tolerance for differences. I know my life was enriched by seeing those four discover and nurture a profound familial connection—a richness of community none of them would have had otherwise.

It always brought tears to June's eyes when she recalled a story Amanda's kindergarten teacher told her. Amanda came into class one day and, with a big smile, announced to her teacher, "I got what I wanted. I got a mommy." Amanda also moved out of Farano House and into June and Stella's home, but she remained close to Barbara.

At about the same time, after many years of renting an apartment, I rented my first house. Barbara helped me pick it out. It was on McKinley Street, about one mile from Farano House. It was a modest place, a small bungalow of red brick. But it was all ours. And the best part of the deal, in Barbara's mind, was that our house was only two blocks from Amanda's new house.

We brought our calico cat, Sweet Pea, and Barbara's gold-fish. I put my foot down when Barbara and Amanda pleaded with me to adopt a mole they found across the street. To my disgust, they brought home for my inspection—possibly just to try to gross me out—various rodents, large insects, and dead birds. They took special delight in seeing me make a queasy face and scream for them to get that critter out of the house.

The girls loved to play with makeup. When they were at Amanda's house, the two managed to get into June's and Stella's makeup with some frequency—covering not only their faces, but their hands and feet, too—in lipstick, blush, eyeliner, and the rest. On one memorable occasion Amanda got into a box of dusting powder at the home of my friend Helen Hayes and came out of the bathroom covered in white powder. Barbara took one look and announced, "Look, Amanda's white now just like me."

A big hill behind an apartment complex near Amanda's house became the girls' special domain. In summer Amanda and Barbara loved to roll down the grassy slope until their clothes were stained a deep shade of emerald. In winter they zipped down the snow-covered hill on plastic saucers, their bright scarves trailing out behind them, their shrieks of joy carried on the icy wind.

As there were for Barbara and me, there were transitions for Amanda and June also. Both June and I were single mothers, although the fact that I was a sister and a member of a religious community cut both ways. Being a sister helped me when it came to a support network, but it complicated matters when it came to societal acceptance and fitting in. The blending of two households—such as June's with what Amanda had known at Farano—is never trouble-free.

For instance, June was quite attached to her West Highland terrier named Daisy. When Amanda moved in, the dog became jealous, but the patient little girl met the dog's occasional snarling with a gentle command: "Stop, Daisy." Amanda and Barbara liked June's cats and our Sweet Pea better.

Barbara sometimes told me about her dream of one day living in a house filled with greyhounds that she would rescue after their racing careers were over. She had learned from Sister Maureen, a dog lover and owner of two pooches, that greyhounds were killed after they were finished racing if they weren't adopted as pets. Barbara was a sensitive soul who showed concern for all creatures great and small.

Over the years Amanda and Barbara became as close as sisters. They took turns eating dinner at each other's house and had regular sleep-overs. Together they went to restaurants, to the movies, to buy new clothes, and to the toy store to get presents. One of their favorite destinations was Hoffman's Playland, a small amusement park in an Albany suburb. The best friends laughed with pure joy as they rode the Tilt-A-Whirl, merry-go-round, miniature train, and Ferris wheel. They enjoyed simple pleasures, too, and loved to go with me to feed bread to the ducks in Albany's Washington Park.

June's job occasionally required travel, and I'd take Amanda for two or three nights during those business trips. That's when Amanda and Barbara became inseparable. Trying to get them to sleep was such a losing battle that I relented and let them both sleep with me in my bed. The two of them slept fine on either side of me, but I resigned myself to a fitful night of slumber.

Because June and I had become close, too, I could rely on her to help me out when I needed it. More significantly, we were able to share the joys and pains of raising a child with HIV and to count on each other for understanding. It was our own sort of support group and a community of caring.

The girls fell into happy seasonal routines. Amanda joined Barbara on our annual summer trips to Cape Cod. They helped plan each other's birthday parties. They hunted for Easter eggs together, went trick-or-treating on Halloween, and opened presents with each other on Christmas. In good weather, they put on impromptu plays for the other children and staff members in the backyard of Farano House. Barbara took the lead, of course, and became playwright, director, producer, and starring actress. Amanda didn't mind and went along with Barbara's stage directions.

They also loved to go shopping together. I remember they liked me to take them to Woolworth's, where they could look around the crowded aisles and I might buy them each a small trinket or two. Amanda's fascination for makeup often led her to the cosmetics counter. During one visit she planted herself at the lipstick display and tried on different shades. Barbara was looking at toys in another aisle, and Amanda called out, "Barb, make your mom buy this pink. To make the boys wink." Such precocious little girls they were.

Barbara and Amanda shared other routines that weren't so carefree. Beginning in the summer of 1989, when both were five years old, the girls spent one morning each month at Albany Medical Center Hospital to have blood drawn for a series of tests. This routine procedure often turned into an ordeal because their veins were so small and difficult to locate. The hospital's staff was wonderful to Barbara and Amanda, whose vibrant presence and special personalities made them something like VIPs on the pediatric wing.

They both loved a particularly playful nurse, who became famous among my family members and friends because she performed "The Vein Dance." This spirited jig made the fear and apprehension disappear in Barbara and Amanda before the needle's stick. The girls also came to know the staff by name and had their favorites. One was a phlebotomist named Ray; he could work magic with their tiny veins. If somebody else was on duty for the blood draw and had trouble finding a vein, Barbara would tell the nurse in charge, "Just go get Ray. Ray can do it every time."

As regular hospital patients Barbara and Amanda made the best of the situation by wearing matching Little Mermaid T-shirt and shorts sets. The two shared the same bed during the hospital procedures, sucked their thumbs, and cuddled as they watched *The Little Mermaid* videos—Barbara had the entire collection—and debated over who got to select the next one.

As they watched a video and picked at the food on their breakfast trays, liquid dripped from a soft bag, down a tube, and into their arms. They always said it looked like milk and that it didn't hurt too much. They pantomimed the procedure with Barbara's beloved Goofy stuffed animal, pretending to stick a needle in the doll's arm, while telling Goofy not to be scared. They finished by placing a Band-Aid on Goofy's arm.

Even the girls' playacting involving the intravenous gamma globulin transfusions was painful for June and me to watch, our minds always fast-forwarding to what these procedures might be like when their symptoms worsened. The girls liked to giggle over the sound of the name of the medication they couldn't pronounce. Gamma globulin. They couldn't fit their mouths around the words and didn't understand the concept of how the cloudy liquid that flowed into their veins for three or four hours was supposed to build up their weakened immune systems by forming antibodies to fight infections.

But Barbara expressed a remarkably developed ability for insight that was far beyond that of most little girls. This gift revealed itself in the imaginative scenarios and stories Barbara created. They were a kind of subconscious peek into her soul. On one hospital visit Barbara offered this allegory to my nieces. Using her stuffed Goofy and a spit bucket to enliven her tale, Barbara said she envisioned that Goofy was sick and that the bucket was a hot-air balloon that would fly to Jupiter, where Goofy would find a Good Witch who would remove the spell that was making him ill.

Another time Barbara told one of my nieces about a dream she had. In her dream she was at an ocean beach gazing out at the breaking surf, when she saw her mommy in heaven in the waves. She walked into the waves to join her mommy in heaven. I was convinced, along with my nieces, that as early as age five, Barbara knew at some subconscious level that she was different because of a deadly virus, even if she could not at that time give a name to her disease.

Barbara was blessed with a skilled and deeply caring physician, Dr. Kallanna Manjunath, a staff pediatrician at Albany Medical Center Hospital—where Barbara received her gamma globulin infusions and other treatments—and later at St. Peter's Hospital in Albany. Dr. Manjunath and his wife, Cathy, formerly an emergency room nurse at St. Peter's Hospital, became like part of our extended family and spent a lot of time at Farano House and at my home with Barbara. Dr. Manjunath has since become a member of the board at CMS.

Also significant in Barbara's medical care was Dr. Nancy Wade, of Albany Medical Center, a pediatrician and specialist in infectious diseases. Dr. Wade made two visits to our house for long and detailed discussions with Barbara about her condition. Barbara had many questions, and I helped her write them down before the visits so she wouldn't forget anything. I had complete confidence in the medical decisions of these two physicians, and they in turn respected the emotional needs of both Barbara and me as we tried to tread that fine line between appropriate care and invasive treatment.

At one point Dr. Manjunath discussed with me experimental AIDS clinical trials being conducted at the time through the National Institutes of Health (NIH) in Washington, D.C. After our discussion and much soul-searching, I decided to forgo the experimental route at NIH and to have Barbara continue to be treated by Dr. Manjunath and Dr. Wade in Albany. My primary concern was not wanting to disturb the happy, normal childhood Barbara enjoyed, or to uproot her from the strong support network of family and friends—and, of course, her best friend, Amanda.

Both doctors were limited in their treatment options for

Barbara in that era's small arsenal of weapons in the fight against pediatric HIV and AIDS: AZT, DDI, Bactrim, and gamma globulin. Each of these medications had potential side effects, of course, and Barbara was particularly prone to the gastrointestinal problems associated with the drugs. She also suffered the added complication of a parasite in her stomach (*crypto sporidia*) that caused nausea and weight loss, adding to her nutritional deficiencies and poor eating habits.

I talked once with Dr. Manjunath in private after he had finished one of Barbara's routine checkups. She had taken the latest news—it was rarely encouraging—with her usual aplomb. Dr. Manjunath marveled at how grounded Barbara was and how she accepted her medical diagnosis from a place of utter faith in God's will. "She has much more insight into chronic illness than most children her age," Dr. Manjunath told me. "She is very courageous and truly stoic. She has faced every aspect of her disease with remarkable courage and determination." Witnessing this little girl's deep well of trust and belief gave us all a valuable life lesson.

Dr. Manjunath went on to praise my work as a mother in helping Barbara battle her disease, which made me feel a little better in the face of additional discouraging news regarding her condition. And then he made a remark that was interesting and insightful for me to ponder. "I don't see you two as having the typical mother-daughter relationship," Dr. Manjunath said. "It's more like two best friends living together, supporting each other. You're both deeply in tune with each other, and as her mother you understand the need to try to balance Barbara's medical needs with her emotional and other needs. That's helping her maintain her quality of life."

The regular visits to Dr. Manjunath's office, monthly blood draws, and gamma globulin infusions carried through the seasons. The fall of 1989 seemed to arrive with unusual haste. It signaled the start of kindergarten for Barbara, another important passage in her life. Amanda stayed at St. Mary's while Barbara began at a new school, Doane Stuart, a highly regarded private prep school. My friend Father Chris was chaplain at the school and had helped arrange a meeting for me with the lower-school principal, Marylou McGurl.

We discussed Barbara's HIV status and came to a consensus. By then medical research had confirmed that there was no way the virus could be spread among children playing and interacting normally at school. But Doane Stuart officials had the same concern about parental fears as had those at St. Mary's. Confidentiality was the key once more, so only the principal was told about Barbara's HIV status.

None of those concerns touched Barbara, who was wrapped up in the excitement of preparing for her first day at kindergarten. I bought her a first-day-of-school dress decorated with a red apple and ABCs. I took her to get a new haircut, a cute little wedge that I thought made her look like the ice skater Dorothy Hamill. Barbara picked out a shiny new Beauty and the Beast lunch box and backpack. She brought a Goofy sleeping bag for naptime. We packed her favorite sandwich, heart-shaped bologna on white bread.

Even brand-new school supplies couldn't take away the jitters of the first day of kindergarten. Barbara began to cry when I told her it was time for me to leave. She clung to my legs and then sobbed as I walked away down the hallway, even with me stopping every few steps to blow kisses. When I came to pick her up, Barbara's teacher told me she'd had a rough first day. When we got in the car, Barbara burst into tears.

"I didn't want you to leave," she said. "I was afraid you'd never come back. Like my mommy in heaven."

This was the mother-daughter dance—two steps forward and one step back. I pulled into the nearest restaurant, my way of trying to overcome my guilt and Barbara's sadness. Howard Johnson's was just down the road from the school, and we ordered ice cream and ate it so fast it gave us headaches. We laughed and made up silly songs. It made Barbara forget her fear, and I felt better too.

After a few days Barbara adjusted to kindergarten and told me she liked it. She was happy at Doane Stuart. Barbara made a lot of friends and felt like one of them. Not an outsider any-more. It may have been the first time in her life where she just blended in, which is all she really wanted. But she didn't tell the other students her secret, and they didn't ask. She remained sensitive about being so tiny, though. Her eating habits and her illness kept her as skinny as a waif. She was the littlest one in her kindergarten class, a position she retained throughout elementary school. I remember that dur-ing her kindergarten year she liked me to read her a book called *The Smallest Boy*. It reinforced a valuable lesson for Barbara: with pluck and perseverance, the smallest can be the greatest.

Gradually Barbara came to realize that size didn't matter, and she found her place among her classmates at school.

With her friend Asia, for instance, she loved to play a game called Brain Quest. Barbara was also the best hair braider at school, according to Casey, who always sought out Barbara to fix her braids just right. Casey shared Barbara's reticence in a group, and they could always be found at the end of the line awaiting recess, happy to avoid the pushing and jostling at the front.

Barbara's heart belonged to Jonathan, though. He was the object of her first serious schoolgirl crush. A sweet boy, he held her hand at a Christmas reception as Barbara, clad in a festive holiday dress, beamed. They giggled together, and Barbara's laugh was a magnet, drawing to her with its effervescence children and adults alike.

Some days I tried as a treat to leave work early in the afternoon and pick up Barbara myself, rather than sending somebody else, as I did when I was tied up in meetings. I was blessed with good friends and wonderful staff members who offered to pick up Barbara from school if work commitments made it impossible for me to get away. As the end of the school day neared on those occasions, I waited at the top of the stairs with the other mothers. When Barbara spotted me, she let out a loud yell from down below that echoed throughout the stairwell: "Mommy! You're here!" Then she ran into my open arms. The other mothers smiled, and I caught their reaction from the corner of my eye. Goose bumps rose on my neck and my face flushed, but not from embarrassment or shame this time. At such moments it didn't feel strange anymore to be both a mother and a sister; it felt good and true. I was reacting now out of pride.

The kindergarten year passed happily, but I started getting

anxious as another legal step approached. Given all Barbara and I had been through, this bit of legal procedure seemed oddly anticlimactic. But it was huge. I applied for formal adoption. I was taking my parenting—and my request from the Sisters of Mercy—to another level, but it seemed inevitable. I had known from the beginning that Barbara and I were not a temporary solution or a momentary fix. Our mother-daughter bond was forever, and I wanted to formalize it.

The Sisters of Mercy had concerns, of course. Adoption meant making a sister a mother permanently, without the disclaimers of foster care. I was impatient and unwavering by this point, wearing my reputation as a nonconformist on my sleeve. I let Sister Karen and the leadership team know that I deeply appreciated the risks they had taken in granting me my request to journey down an uncharted road as a foster parent. In the next breath, I reiterated my position that this profound bond Barbara and I had established could not possibly be broken at this point. I was prepared to leave the Sisters of Mercy if there was no other way I could adopt Barbara. There was no mistaking where I stood in my resolve to become Barbara's legal mother and to make her my daughter. Period. No "foster kid" tag to go with it. I didn't feel like I was making a threat. Rather, it was a statement of fact. I hadn't felt this strongly about anything else in my life, and I was absolutely committed to making sure that nothing would break the mother-daughter connection between Barbara and me.

Of course there was some lingering opposition within my religious community that carried through from my foster care request. I had another meeting with the leadership team. More canon lawyers were consulted. The bishop reiterated his support. It was more or less a repeat of the earlier procedure. The stakes were higher, however, and not only for me.

Afterward, regional president Sister Karen told me that my passionate statement had swung the pendulum in my favor. The leadership team members were in agreement that I had been a full and active participant in my religious community while taking care of Barbara as her foster mother and that I was too valuable a member to force to leave by denying my request for formal adoption. At that point, without further delay, my request for adoption was approved.

It takes a village to raise a child, it's been said, and that's roughly how many of Barbara's friends and supporters accompanied me to Putnam County for the adoption ceremony on October 23, 1990. We filled a van and several cars followed. June and Amanda and several members of my family came.

It's funny, but the first thing I thought about when we got there was that the benches in Family Court looked and felt like church pews. In a way this was another kind of final vows for me. I closed my eyes and considered the parallels. This day's ceremony recalled for me the joining of myself to Jesus Christ through my vows as a sister, symbolized with a silver ring. Similarly there was ritual and a lifelong commitment made this day. Before a judge, Barbara and I pledged ourselves to each other as mother and daughter. I was overcome with emotion and cried. I'm not sure if there was a dry eye in the courtroom.

I don't think I'd ever been happier or more proud. A room off the court had been decorated with balloons by the social-services staff at Putnam County. Everyone brought a dish to share for a potluck meal, and there were a bouquet of roses and many presents for Barbara. It was a joyous celebration, and I didn't want that moment of elation to end.

The party wound down, though, and I drove back to Albany with Barbara. We were surprised to find our house filled with more flowers, balloons, and presents. We stayed up late to bake cupcakes for Barbara to bring to school the next day.

Barbara was six years old now and recently had been seeing TV programs about HIV and AIDS. She was beginning to ask more questions. And I was struggling to give answers that satisfied her.

Chapter Nine

Coping With Illness

I've never liked confrontation. Don't get me wrong. It's not that I'm not a forceful presence when it comes to running CMS and fighting for my staff, our clients, and what they need. It's just that when it comes to personal issues, I find it easier to go around dilemmas. For as long as possible I tend to avoid facing the inevitably difficult and demanding work of looking inward and coming to terms with a problem. Travel offers that kind of avoidance; that's how I ended up taking Barbara to Disney World.

Off and on throughout the summer and fall of 1991, Barbara had been asking me to take her to Disney World. Remembering the strain of earlier trips, I hesitated because I didn't think she was strong enough. She now suffered from constant fatigue and diarrhea. In her weakened, sickly condition, I worried whether she'd even enjoy Disney World. There was also the matter of paying for it.

Our friend Father Tony stepped in. He said he'd been saving some money for a special present, and he wanted to give Barbara a trip to Disney World as a gift for their friendship. He was blunt with me: "I don't think we should wait."

I had always respected Tony's guidance. In fact, he was my counselor and we talked friend to friend, spiritual adviser to client, family supporter to mother. I admitted that I was trying to deny my daughter's illness. I listened to Tony's wisdom. Barbara, Tony, and I booked a flight to Florida.

Barbara's fatigue remained a constant presence. The diarrhea followed her on vacation, too, a most trying situation. She was embarrassed when she had an accident, but nothing darkened the bright, shining world of Disney for Barbara. Tony and I took turns pushing Barbara in a stroller. Nobody paid us any notice. Others didn't realize they were witnessing a most unusual trio: a priest, a sister, and her daughter. We went on many kiddie rides together, twirling in teacups and galloping on merry-go-rounds. We took a lot of pictures.

A friend of Tony's got us special access to the Disney characters. Barbara loved it and we took snapshots of her with Mickey Mouse and Goofy—Goofy was still her favorite character. We vowed not to let HIV and AIDS get in the way of our joy together. Time stood still at Disney World. It was as if these moments of joy were frozen in a rainbow of hope and beauty. We were very happy, but one thing was missing.

Barbara had a request. "Mommy, can I call Tony 'Daddy'?"

The little girl had never known her biological father, who died of AIDS soon after he was released from prison. I looked at Tony. We both paused and then nodded. For a time, at least, in the land of make-believe that was Disney World,

Barbara had all the family she ever wanted.

I have many pictures of Tony, Barbara, and me together at Disney World—a trio of big smiles, with Barbara's little crooked tooth on the right side protruding. If you look at the pictures closely, however, her skin appears sallow and pulls back thin and tight from the mouth. It's obvious in the photographs that she was sick and getting sicker. My denials couldn't change that.

Later that fall, after returning from Disney World, I knew the time had come for what I had always imagined in my mind as "the big conversation." This defining moment occurred when Barbara was seven years old and a second grader at Doane Stuart School. Her health had become a constant concern, and Barbara had been prescribed drugs to combat the AIDS symptoms. Barbara had to drink the medication in the principal's office at school, and she hated everything about it: having to leave her friends behind in the classroom, having to feel different and like an outsider again. Once while she was putting up her usual arguments and delaying tactics before taking her medicine, a little boy said he wanted to try some. "OK, you can have it all," Barbara said. A nice try on Barbara's part, but that was a no-go.

Nothing could dampen my daughter's playfulness, but results of Barbara's recent blood tests had made her doctors very concerned. Her T-cell count, a prime indicator of the strength of the immune system, was dropping sharply. Doctors prescribed AZT, a drug that had shown promise in HIV patients. Its hope came at the cost of a difficult regimen. I had to wake up Barbara in the middle of the night and have her drink the AZT, a clear liquid that was at least mostly tasteless. Groggy and disoriented from being awakened from a sound sleep, Barbara balked. I tried everything to get Barbara to swallow the medication. She kept asking why she needed to take so much medicine. The other kids at school didn't have to. Barbara questioned me more and more, and my answers were becoming increasingly feeble and less believable.

In fact, Barbara surely could sense I was evading her questions. It was time to stop the evasion. I knew the moment had come for the conversation I had long dreaded. I tried to deny it, and every day I told myself that maybe the disease would skip over Barbara. I began to pray daily for nothing short of a miracle. But the disease marched on.

Thanksgiving was approaching, and we had put up our decorations and begun our preparations—those little rituals of the holidays Barbara and I had developed on our own. I finally summoned my courage and decided there could be no more delays. On an ordinary night in November, while Barbara was taking a bath—a place of comfort where she loved to linger, the location for many philosophical discussions—she got on the topic of death and her mother. Barbara asked me question after question about how her mother died, and she wouldn't accept my evasions any longer. I had never deliberately lied to her, but I had consciously avoided offering information and carefully sidestepped her queries. But Barbara had me here. She had been learning a lot about HIV and AIDS and put the question to me point-blank. The timing was right.

I took a deep breath and began to speak without knowing precisely what I would say. "Barbara? Remember when you asked me about HIV just now? And remember when I told you your mommy in heaven had HIV?"

Barbara's eyes narrowed and her little face folded into a frown. "She did?" Barbara asked. She wouldn't break her piercing stare. It seemed to bore into my heart. "How do people get HIV?"

"There are a few ways you can get it," I said. "Everybody does things in life they're sorry they did. That's what happened with your mommy. And that's how she got HIV."

"Did you always know my mommy had HIV?"

I nodded silently.

Barbara's eyes flared and the frown turned into a scowl. "Why didn't you tell me? I'm really mad at you. You're my mommy. You should have told me."

"Well, you were very young," I said. "I didn't think you'd understand what I meant. So I waited until you were older."

Barbara glared and was silent. She was giving me the daggers look. I couldn't bring myself to meet her gaze. I looked at the bathroom floor and stumbled along.

"I need to tell you one more thing about your mommy in heaven. I told you she had HIV. There's another way you can get HIV that I didn't tell you about before. If someone's mommy has HIV and she has a baby, lots of times the baby is born with HIV. And that's what happened with you."

Barbara was quiet now and looked stunned. It felt like the air had been sucked out of the room. Barbara sat motionless for a long moment. She may have previously sensed subconsciously this intersection between HIV, her mother, and herself, but she had never heard it plainly spoken. I shot her glances and stared at the bathwater slowly losing its bubbles.

Barbara's voice was soft and flat when she finally spoke.

"So you're telling me I have HIV."

Barbara's round face, her almond-shaped eyes, and the damp auburn hair all went blurry through my tears. They pooled up in my eyes and ran down my cheeks.

It was Barbara who broke the painful silence. "How long did you know?"

"Since I met you."

"I can't believe you didn't tell me," Barbara said. "Why? I'm never going to trust you again."

I tried to explain again to Barbara that she was so young, and I didn't think it was appropriate or that she could have understood about HIV at that point. Besides, she was healthy and happy then. It was a mother's hope, I suppose, a mother's denial, although I didn't articulate that.

Barbara refused to sit still for the rest of the explanation. She asked for her bath towel, wrapped herself, and silently walked past me into her bedroom, closing the door behind her. I didn't say anything or try to stop her. I went into the living room, sat on the sofa, and let the tears come.

Barbara came into the living room in her pajamas a short time later, and I wiped my eyes. Her anger had subsided, replaced with curiosity. "Does Amanda have HIV too?" Barbara asked. I paused. I had been discussing with June this very situation just the other day. June had not yet had this conversation with Amanda. I was torn over deciding what was the best way to handle Barbara's question and, in the end, went with my heart.

"Barbara, honey, you're a smart little girl," I said. "Yes, Amanda has HIV. But her mommy hasn't told her yet. It's very private information. Do you understand that? This part is very important. It's nobody's business. It's a family matter that we keep in the family and don't tell anybody else."

"Well, I'm going to tell Amanda I have HIV," Barbara said.

"That's OK," I said. "She's your best friend, and we consider Amanda part of our family. But it's not something you should tell the kids at school or anyone else who's not in our family."

That constant vigilance and fearfulness of the secret getting out was a terrible burden for a little girl. Barbara tried to talk her way out of this code of silence with some of my staff members, who also knew her HIV status. "How come I can't tell my teachers, if they're supposed to be so smart?" Barbara asked Tracie Killar, the AIDS education coordinator at Farano House. Barbara spoke with Tracie about how she struggled to keep the secret and her constant fear that somebody at her school would find out. "Maybe the HIV will spill out from my body and the other kids will see it and know I've got it," Barbara told Tracie.

Barbara showed remarkable poise and discipline for her age when it came to keeping the secret. She kept it in the family. But newspapers and network TV, even Nickelodeon, the children's cable channel, carried many stories about people dying of AIDS. Barbara watched these shows with interest. One night after such a program she had questions for me.

"I know HIV leads to AIDS. That's what my mommy in heaven died from. I'm afraid I'm going to get AIDS," Barbara said.

I was successful in changing the topic. Barbara lost interest in her line of questioning. I just couldn't face that next phase of the discussion right now. Christmas had arrived, and

I didn't want disease and grim realities to intrude upon and overshadow the holiday spirit.

Barbara had a big surprise awaiting her under the tree on Christmas morning. It was a pink Barbie Corvette convertible. It was the kind you sit in and drive, with a gas pedal, brakes, a steering wheel, and a rechargeable battery. It cost a lot, but just let somebody criticize me for spoiling my daughter. I didn't care. Barbara loved the Barbie Corvette and drove the pink convertible over to Amanda's house Christmas morning.

Christmas came and went in a blur of presents and excitement, but I couldn't get a dark thought out of my head. I didn't share my fear with anyone, not even when it wouldn't go away. The fear I dared not express was this: Would this be my daughter's last Christmas?

The Barbie sports car was a big hit. I couldn't get Barbara out of the driver's seat—not until she got her first bike that spring. It was pink and purple, with glittery streamers dangling from the handlebars. I had picked out the flashiest one I could find. Barbara wobbled back and forth on training wheels along the sidewalk to Amanda's house. I huffed behind, helping Barbara steer and giving her a little push up the inclines.

I made her wear a helmet, and she argued as if I were making her eat broccoli at dinner. But on this matter I wouldn't give in, and I refused to answer her complaints. She put on the helmet and kept it on. Barbara soon wanted me to take off the training wheels. I resisted at first. She said I was no fun, that I was too protective and treated her like a baby. She was a big girl and ready for a two-wheeler. I pretended not to watch when Father Tony came over and took off the training wheels. With Tony trotting behind, Barbara rode free on two wheels. I watched from the sidewalk as she giggled and shrieked with joy.

"Mommy! I feel like I'm flying. Just like in my dreams!"

That summer the blood tests detected a problem. The AZT treatment apparently had lost its effectiveness. Barbara's T-cell count had dropped dangerously low. For a long time her T-cell counts had been in the 900- to 1,000-range. That was an adequate T-cell count and meant that Barbara's body could fight off infection. Suddenly her count plummeted to below 500. She was at risk. Doctors immediately switched her medicine from AZT to a different antiviral drug called DDI, which had just been approved for children. In trials with kids DDI had shown positive results, apparently without serious side effects.

Barbara's diarrhea had become chronic by this time, and it was a very difficult period. Her already poor appetite faded, and she felt tired and weak practically all the time. Her beloved pink Barbie Corvette and the bike were parked in the garage to gather dust. Doctors were concerned about her gastrointestinal complications, which could mean that she had crossed a threshold in the advance of the disease, shifting from a three-letter virus to the fearsome four-letter syndrome.

Barbara celebrated her eighth birthday in the summer of 1992, though it was a subdued celebration. Autumn followed quickly. She entered third grade but had difficulty focusing on school. The winter was longer and darker than usual because of Barbara's declining condition. She longed for springtime's return.

Without warning, a chance to help spring arrive early came our way. Our friend Sister Maureen was a presenter at a conference for social-service agency directors in Albuquerque, and she invited Barbara and me to join her. In the early months of 1993, with Barbara's health getting worse by the week, the warmth and sunshine of New Mexico sounded like just the antidote to a cold and gloomy Albany winter.

Barbara's illness required special planning before the trip. I had her medications prepared for the plane ride and arranged to have a pharmacist near our hotel in Albuquerque fill her prescriptions and deliver them to the hotel. The long flight was difficult for Barbara as the diarrhea forced her to make countless trips to the bathroom. I held her hand and walked with her each time, which tested the patience of us both.

The hotel had very nice amenities, including a great out-door pool. The weather was warm and sunny, and Barbara loved sitting in the sun poolside, trying to muster her queenly regalness and her enjoyment at being addressed as "darlink." She wasn't feeling well, though, and we soon gave up trying to be silly just for silliness' sake and fell into the drowsy, silent pleasure of soaking up the sun. We went back to the room so I could help Barbara take her meds, only to discover that the refrigerator had been unplugged. I flipped out and let fly a stream of less-than-exemplary language. I was angry with myself for not checking the refrigerator first before we left and mad at the hotel staff for unplugging it. But Barbara's calmness and patience shone through, and she helped me regain my composure quickly.

Worried that the prescriptions had spoiled, I called up the pharmacy and told them about the situation. The pharmacist was understanding and helpful and sent an employee over with a new order right away. Barbara had assured me everything would be OK, and it was.

In hindsight, though, the trip to Albuquerque might have been too ambitious. It wore both of us out, and the return flight was interminable as I came down with a horrible stomach virus. I groaned and slept my way cross-country in a feverish haze. Luckily Maureen stepped in and took care of Barbara on the return flight, assuming my place on the endless trips to the bathroom.

I got home and collapsed into bed. That bug devastated me. It was unusual for me to be sick enough to stay home from work. Barbara was acting strangely, too, but it had nothing to do with her physical health. I managed to get her to open up about what was wrong, and she told me she was afraid I was getting sick like her mommy in heaven and that I was going to die, too. I held her close and promised her that mine was only a temporary illness. Her mood improved when I made a quick recovery and got out of bed and back to my routine the following day.

I stopped taking pictures of Barbara after the Albuquerque trip. I couldn't bear the images of illness. What lay ahead was another country. We were strangers in that land of disease, and we feared the place.

Chapter Ten

Embracing Life, Accepting Death

B arbara and Amanda, best friends through thick and thin, got sicker together in the spring of 1993. Their symptoms mirrored each other's. Both girls grew progressively weaker and complained of being tired all the time. When it became necessary to hospitalize them, they were given adjacent rooms. It was during this hospitalization that Amanda lost her eyesight.

While they were in the hospital, the girls watched videos together—their favorites were *Beethoven*, *Sister Act*, and *Heidi*—and Barbara offered a running commentary to compensate for Amanda's blindness. Barbara captured the spirit of each story. The two girls laughed in the same spots. Barbara also brought along some of her favorite books, including the Ramona series, which was very special to us. A friend of mine told me how, trying to be helpful, she had started to read a Ramona book to Barbara, but Barbara cut her off. "Oh,

153

no," Barbara said. "Only Mommy can read me those."

Both girls received many treatments and procedures—a continuous flow of more and different drugs and additional tests. However, though a mother's love is blind, it gradually became apparent that there was no cure happening here and it was only a matter of time.

I watched the events unfold in numb terror as Barbara literally began wasting away before my eyes. I agonized over the decision but eventually gave doctors approval to install a central feeding line in her chest. Intravenous feedings were supposed to give her strength and help her gain back weight. The central feeding line was a last-ditch effort that didn't have much effect. The rational side of my brain knew we were grasping at straws here, but we were praying for a miracle. When your eight-year-old daughter is dying, you'll try to cling to any shred of hope you can find. Prayer, at least, provided a ray of optimism.

Eventually Barbara was discharged from the hospital, while Amanda remained there as a patient. I finally agreed to accept the recommendation of Dr. Manjunath, who said that there was nothing more they could do medically for Barbara. He said that she was not responding to treatment and was only going to get sicker day by day. He suggested home would be the best place for her, with her mommy. I was running on adrenaline at this point and hardly remember driving Barbara home to our house on McKinley Street. I do recall the date. It was Good Friday.

A few months earlier my brother-in-law Art, in the advanced stages of lung cancer, had been hospitalized. Barbara loved Art, and they had a special bond, sharing the experience of illness and much more. Before he became gravely ill, I would drop off Barbara at Art and my sister Mela's house, just a few blocks from my office. Art would hold Barbara in his lap and tell her stories, or they'd watch TV together. Art was sick and weak at this point and tired easily, but Barbara had a special empathy for Art's illness. Art in turn offered a grandfatherly presence to Barbara.

Gradually Art's cancer progressed, his condition became critical, and we were told that death was near. Barbara pleaded with me to take her to the hospital to see Art, but I tried to discourage it because she was so weak herself and I thought seeing Art that way might frighten her. Barbara wouldn't let it go, however, and argued and pushed my buttons. I finally relented when Art scrawled in a note that he would like to see Barbara.

Barbara did not show the least bit of fear when she entered Art's hospital room. She was used to a hospital's tubes and machines, the nurses and doctors, the sights and smells. She sat down in a chair next to Art's bed and stroked his hand and arm near his IV. "I know that hurts," she said. "Look at my black and blues." She held up her arm to reveal her IV marks. Barbara whispered to Art about how tired and weak she was, too. Tears flowed from Art's closed eyes. Nobody tried to wipe them away. She spoke to Art as if nobody else were in the room—just them, one on one. After a short visit she said it was time for her to go. She leaned over, stroked Art's cheek, kissed it, and said, "'Bye, Art. I love you." For the first time in hours, Art opened his eyes and mouthed "I love you" to Barbara.

Art passed away in March, and Barbara wanted to go to the

funeral. I didn't object at all this time. She was sick and uncomfortable throughout the service, too sick to stand or kneel. I cradled her on my lap, distracted with my own thoughts. The thing I couldn't get out of my head was, the next funeral we'll all be attending will be Barbara's.

Barbara had missed many weeks of school during her hospitalization that spring. She'd been in third grade when she became too ill to continue. She slept most of the time at home, and the simple effort of speaking wore her out. Still, she was invited to the last day of class and graduation ceremonies in early June.

Barbara had always summoned deep reserves of strength when she needed them, and this was such a time. "Mommy, I'd like to go to graduation," she said. I started to say no and to explain my reasons for not allowing it, but I'd seen that look in Barbara's green eyes before. It was the flaring of fight and determination, and I had learned not to stand in the way of it. I nodded my head yes, and the slight crease of a smile— the first in many days—spread across Barbara's gaunt face.

The preparations were a welcome distraction. Still the little princess, Barbara went through her closet, searching for the right outfit. She brought out several dresses. She tried on a few, but she'd lost so much weight that they hung loosely on her. She finally settled on a long-sleeve cotton flower-print dress, and she asked my sister-in-law to make the necessary alterations. I felt anxious and didn't think this was a good idea, but I had come to understand Barbara's need for closure—as with the birthday party for her mommy in heaven. Something deep in Barbara required her to be in attendance on the last day of school and to participate in graduation ceremonies. She needed to finish that part of her journey. I offered my encouragement and support.

When we got to the front door of Doane Stuart School, Barbara paused and looked scared. She said she had changed her mind and wanted to go back to the car and go home. I held her hand and talked about how much she had been looking forward to this day and that it would be a shame to turn back now. I offered to pick her up and carry her into her classroom, but Barbara refused. Slowly, haltingly, she shuffled to her classroom door. It was painful for me to see her, all skin and bone, weighing about thirty pounds.

Barbara paused at the door. I stood at her side and could see tears welling up in her eyes. "Mommy, I don't think I can go in. They'll see how sick I look and run away."

I told Barbara she had come for a purpose and that everything would be all right. I told her I would be waiting for her right outside. I held the door open for Barbara, and she moved tentatively into the classroom.

The boy Barbara had called her boyfriend was the first to come over. He helped Barbara to her desk, and she sat down. The precise nature of her condition had remained a secret to the kids at Doane Stuart. Remarkably, her classmates did not pry and accepted her as she was. Her friends did not act any differently toward her. They smiled and greeted her warmly. I watched from the classroom door and could see from Barbara's grin that she felt welcome and at peace.

The final class ended and her classmates crowded around Barbara. They talked and laughed, discussed plans for the summer, and said their goodbyes. Some of them hugged her, and she basked in the attention.

We all went to chapel for the closing ceremonies, and I sat in the back pew with Barbara, who said she didn't feel well. This was the same chapel where Barbara had drawn smiles just a year earlier by playing air guitar with joyous abandon during the musical selections at services. Barbara's health had declined so abruptly that it was difficult to think she was so gravely ill now. Seeing her discomfort, I told her we could leave before the ceremonies were over, but she said she wanted to hear her name called. We waited until the principal called out, "Barbara Elaine LoGiudice," signaling that she had completed third grade.

In the days following graduation Barbara's decline hastened. She became very lethargic and stopped speaking. She would only moan or groan when I changed the sheets or her clothes. She was sleeping in my queen-sized bed now. I barely slept and lost track of the time, whether it was night or day. I cried through the dark and existed only in the rhythms of Barbara's illness.

On Sunday Barbara was too weak to go to church, and I decided it was time for another big conversation. I sat her on my lap on the sofa. This time I didn't dread the big conversation. We had come through so much together, and there was no more time for secrets.

"Barbara, you know a lot about HIV. And you have HIV. And you know people with HIV sooner or later have AIDS. And that's what has happened to you."

"Are you telling me I have AIDS?"

"Yes, honey."

"Are you telling me I'm going to die?"

"We tried so hard. You've fought so long. The doctors did

everything they could do. But you've gotten sicker and sicker. That's what happens to people with AIDS. No matter how much you love them, how hard everyone tries, they don't get better and they die."

The only sound was that of a mother's and daughter's muffled crying, enveloped in each other's embrace. I let the tears and the silence wash over us for several long minutes before I spoke. "I just bought some new photo albums. Let's go through our pictures and take out our favorite ones. Then we'll put them in our new albums."

Barbara became absorbed in the photos and the flood of memories they brought on. Every picture had a story.

"Mommy, don't worry," Barbara said. "Don't be sad. I think God wants me to have a long life. I'm just a little girl. God doesn't want me to die yet."

Later that day, June and Amanda came over to our house. They had barely settled in before Barbara, seated in her child-sized recliner chair, asked, "June, did you know I had AIDS and you didn't tell me?" June was caught off guard, and she looked over at me as her eyes welled up with tears. June had not found the right time to have the big conversation with Amanda yet. Before June could compose herself and say something in reply, Barbara blurted out that Amanda had AIDS, too.

June and I always suspected that these two bright and curi-ous eight-year-olds knew more than they cared to verbalize. As mothers we knew Amanda and Barbara talked to each other often in private about HIV. They had gone to counsel-ing sessions together, after all, and June and I both realized the need to give the girls some private space.

Barbara's utterance in the living room—as stunned as it left us at first—actually worked to clear the air. We expected a storm and experienced a soothing calm instead. Amanda and Barbara quickly lost interest in questioning us as mothers and instead turned their attention to the pictures we had just placed in the new photo albums. Amanda was blind, but she enjoyed Barbara's commentary on each image. The best friends lingered over the many pictures of themselves together.

Within days Barbara needed new, powerful drugs to block her severe pain. The doctors prescribed morphine to be administered directly through the central line in her chest. Bottled oxygen helped her breathe. Time seemed to stand still, and I felt like I was in a fog as friends and family—the village that helped me raise Barbara—spent time with the little girl they had come to love ... the child who had been their teacher.

I hardly noticed the steady stream of visitors through my veil of tears. I lay beside Barbara in bed, caressing her face, singing her soft lullabies, and kissing her head as she slept.

When we were alone, I spoke in a low whisper. I couldn't tell if Barbara still could hear me or whether she understood the words I hoped would bring her comfort. "God loves you," I said. "Heaven is a wonderful place. You won't be sick anymore there. Your mommy in heaven will be waiting for you. You've fought so hard. You don't need to fight anymore. It's time to let go."

It was a Friday night. Two of my close friends, Maureen and Mary Jo, had offered to stay over. They took turns with me, keeping constant vigil over Barbara. I was alone in the room on my bed with Barbara when her breathing grew weak and shallow. On Saturday morning, June 19, 1993, a little after eight o'clock, Barbara stopped breathing. I lay beside my daughter, holding her next to me. At that moment I experienced a kind of warm glow, a sense of inner peace. I wasn't frightened. Barbara died wearing a Little Mermaid nightgown, clutching her favorite stuffed animal, Goofy. My final words to Barbara were, "You're going from a place of love to another place of love."

Barbara was laid to rest in her First Communion dress, with her stuffed Goofy in her arms. Barbara's funeral was held at the Cathedral of the Immaculate Conception in downtown Albany. I was surprised to find the big cathedral nearly full, but it only reinforced what I always knew: the gift of Barbara touched many. The little girl who had arrived in Albany five years before alone, an orphan, had practically packed the place. The several hundred people in attendance followed the service in a program printed on yellow paper. The program's cover had one of Barbara's drawings, the one about her dream that she could fly.

June and Amanda, along with Sister Helen from Farano House and members of my staff, helped prepare the gifts of the Eucharist. Helen Hayes, Sister Maureen Joyce, and Sister Jane McCullough read the Scriptures.

Barbara's Bible was placed on the altar. One of the songs we chose was "We Are the Family." The first verse goes like this: "And in our family all are welcome. It doesn't matter who you are. In our home there's always room, so plan to stay."

Barbara's friend Bishop Howard Hubbard presided, and

her other friends, Father Tony Chiaramonte and Father Chris DeGiovine, joined the bishop in offering the Mass of Christian Burial. Many sisters from my Sisters of Mercy community attended, including a few of those who had opposed my request for adoption. They had become Barbara's friends too. "Our daughter" was how they had taken to referring to Barbara. In turn, Barbara liked to call the elderly sisters in our community "all my grandmothers."

The bishop spoke and captured the essence of Barbara in my life. "The love of Mary Ann, who despite great obstacles—canonical, social, and personal—found a way to provide her 'queen' with a home and family, a place of security, belonging, stability, and loving care."

The bishop recalled fond memories of Barbara. He said he kept a picture of her in his office and carried her memory in his heart. "Barbara's is truly a fantastic love story," he said. "A triumph of the human spirit and the conquest of goodness over the forces of ignorance, fear, sickness, suffering, and even death."

Father Tony, the priest Barbara had asked to pretend to be her daddy at Disney World, delivered the homily. "One of the things I will treasure always is how Barbara helped me to tap into my own inner child," he said. "She helped me to play, to be free, to act like a fool, not to worry about what people are saying.... I treasure Barbara's continual love, constant caring, being able to act like a father figure that I never had the opportunity to realize, yet deeply longed for. Barbara brought a deeper meaning to my life, an intimacy, love, and affection a parent feels."

A poem by Emily Dickinson was printed in the back of

the yellow program. One stanza went like this:

> *A timid thing—to drop a life*
> *Into the mystical well—*
> *Too plummetless—that it come back—*
> *Eternity—until ...*

In the difficult days and weeks that followed, I felt overwhelmed by grief and sorrow and could hardly manage to be present and attentive to the outpouring of love and concern from family members and friends. One conversation I remember being deeply touched by was with Sister Karen Marcil, president of my religious community. "God put that beautiful child in your life for a reason," she told me. "Barbara not only changed your life but touched so many members of our community. Barbara had a wonderfully positive effect on the Sisters of Mercy. We're all here to support you in your time of loss."

Bishop Hubbard made time in his busy schedule to see me that summer. "You were a wonderful mother to Barbara," the bishop told me. "And you broke new ground as far as the Catholic Church is concerned. You were both an inspiration to me. I consider giving my support to your request for becoming Barbara's mother one of the best decisions I've made as bishop. It was the right and just thing to do."

That August Amanda had an opportunity to attend the Double "H" Hole in the Woods Ranch in Lake Luzerne, New York, a program for children with terminal illnesses. Amanda was concerned she would be away for Barbara's ninth birthday on August 18—it didn't seem to matter to Amanda that

Barbara had died. Amanda made her best friend a birthday gift, a yellow, heart-shaped pillow. With her mother's help, Amanda wrote on the pillow the title of their favorite song in yellow glitter glue, "You Are My Sunshine."

Amanda called from camp on Barbara's birthday to speak with me. "I wish Barbara was here," Amanda said. "I think about her every day."

Amanda died the following month, in September 1993.

Amanda's mother, June, died at age forty-four in April 1997 from diabetes and its complications. Amanda and June were buried near Barbara in Our Lady of Angels Cemetery in Colonie, a suburb of Albany.

Barbara's small gravestone has her name, the year of her birth and death, butterflies, and a rainbow carved into the gray granite. Barbara had loved butterflies all her life, and people often gave her toys in the shape of butterflies. The summer before she died, a friend of my niece gave Barbara a unique butterfly gift, an orange monarch in its cocoon. Barbara kept it in a jar in the kitchen and looked at it every day. Then it turned black and she got scared. She was very upset and cried that the butterfly had died. She told my niece, who was taking care of her, that she had to call Mommy at work. I could hear the sense of panic in Barbara's voice and rushed home.

When I got there, the butterfly had already emerged and was drying its wings. I held Barbara's hands as the butterfly took flight. "See, Mommy, I made sure it didn't fly before you got home," she said. Her fear had turned into elation. The seasons, the cycle of life, the mystery of God's plan, went on.

Father Michael Farano, for whom Farano House is named,

commemorated the lives of Barbara and Amanda in his homily on the first Sunday in October 1993. "These two little girls, and those who died before them, have brought so much love and caring into the lives of so many persons that there is no doubt in my mind as to the effectiveness, importance, and inestimable value of their lives. The funerals of these children unfailingly witness to the power of a life. Persons of all backgrounds, races, religions, and professions came to be with them for a final time.... The theme of those who speak is always the same. It is the theme of love; the love which these youngsters were able to give and elicit."

Chapter Eleven

Blessings and Yellow Butterflies

T he following fall, more than a year after Barbara's death, I was still mired in depression. The death of my beloved daughter shattered my faith. I stopped praying altogether, found excuses not to go to church, and wandered through my days at work. Sister Maureen was there for me, always willing to listen as I expressed my sense of anger and profound disappointment over a God who would allow the slow, agonizing death of a beautiful child like Barbara.

Maureen and other close friends gave me their support and made time for me in their busy lives as I tried to come to terms with the heartbreaking loss. Maureen tried to lift my spirits by talking about how much she admired the risk I took in becoming Barbara's mother and how much I had grown as a person. She said she'd observed how I had become more deeply in touch with my emotions as a result of raising Barbara.

As part of the process of struggling to regain my faith and a satisfying spiritual life as a sister, I went on our annual retreat to Weston Priory in Vermont. The retreat director, Sister Jane Silk, encouraged me to let go of Barbara, to try to move beyond the loss. But I remained in a place of darkness and sadness. I wrote in my journal about how I could not come to closure over her death, and how nothing else in my life mattered. The retreat was nearly finished and had been largely a waste of time in my mind.

On the final day I awoke to an unusually warm, bright, and sunny October morning. I walked to a pond behind our retreat house, soothed by the solitude and silence. The pond is where Barbara and I had spent many hours observing nature. Just then two yellow butterflies fluttered over the water, and I closed my eyes. My mind filled with images of Barbara, of the monarch butterfly that had not died, and about Barbara's dreams of flying. I recalled so many happy times together—Disney World and walks in the park and how Barbara said goodbye for the last time. She was very concerned about me and said that I should not be sad when she was gone. She promised to watch over me and said we'd be together one day in heaven.

I lost all sense of time or place beside that pond and felt as peaceful and free as when I floated on my back in the sea at Cape Cod. The sun hurt my eyes when I opened them again. Now a dozen yellow butterflies were taking flight above the pond, and I heard Barbara's laughter in my head, bright and high and happy.

The depression that had gripped me for so long suddenly seemed to release its hold, and I felt an inner peace. Barbara helped me to this place of letting go. As I prepared to leave Weston Priory at the conclusion of our retreat, a yellow butterfly flew near my car, paused, fluttered, rose, and disappeared over the house. I had experienced an epiphany. I knew at that moment that I was a sister and a mother forever, a traveler on the road to redemption. I had come to terms with the short time I had with Barbara as her mother. I believe that our journey together—the heartbreak as much as the joy— was meant to be part of God's plan.

That spring my niece Anne Marie Couser gave birth to a baby daughter, Margaret, whom we call Margie. She has become one of my favorite grandnieces. I volunteer to babysit with Margie. I take her to McDonald's and for walks in the park to feed the ducks. She's my date for Walt Disney movies. Margie likes to stay overnight at my house, and when I'm getting her ready for bed, I tell her stories about Barbara. Margie likes it when I take out the photo albums and show her pictures of my daughter and tell her about what we did when Barbara was Margie's age.

It took plenty of grieving and healing for me to get to this point. There was a long period when I shied away from my grandnieces and grandnephews because it made me think of losing Barbara and it was too painful. Now when little Margie places her tiny hand in mine as we walk, I'm sometimes transported back in time, and it feels like I'm with Barbara again. Never underestimate the power of the blessed innocence and healing touch of a child to revive one's spirits.

My family was deeply touched and changed forever by Barbara. My nieces often remind me that they believe Barbara is watching over them and making her presence felt. For instance, one niece, Marialyce Lyons, had been waiting for years to adopt a child. Five years after Barbara's death, she got a call about a woman pregnant with twins who planned to give the babies to an adoptive mother. The twin girls, Tess and Faye, were born prematurely one day before Barbara's birthday. They're healthy and doing well, having turned one year old over the summer. Also, my niece Patrice Delehanty has a daughter, Kathryn, and she gave her the middle name of Elaine—the same as Barbara's middle name.

I also take heart in knowing that the dedication of my staff at Farano House toward AIDS education, together with the hard work of many other AIDS educators in New York state, has had a positive effect. Statewide, the number of pediatric AIDS cases has been dropping steadily each year over the past decade. I'm encouraged, too, by the fact that children with AIDS are living longer with the disease now than when Barbara died of AIDS in 1993. Since then, effective drug combinations, called "cocktails," have shown excellent results in extending the lives of AIDS patients, as well as improving their overall quality of life as they cope with the disease. Pediatricians treat AIDS nowadays more like a chronic illness, rather than the imminent death sentence it was in the early years of the epidemic.

Not long ago Sister Maureen and I attended the confirmation and Mass of a twelve-year-old boy who had come to Farano House as an HIV-positive infant. As he walked up the church aisle in a crisply pressed suit, she and I brushed back tears of pride and joy. It was the same church where just a few years earlier we had mourned the deaths of young children from Farano House who died of AIDS at a tender age. After the confirmation service, we hugged our Farano alumnus and posed for pictures. He's happy, healthy, and well adjusted. His future is bright, despite his medical diagnosis.

More and more frequently, our Farano kids, diagnosed with HIV at birth, are living into adolescence and beyond. What's more, the public fear and initial hysteria associated with AIDS—a major concern of ours when Barbara arrived at Farano in 1988—have largely subsided. As a result of public understanding and medical improvements for HIV-positive children and their mothers with AIDS, our role at Farano House has shifted. Similar programs that used Farano as a model have since become available in New York City, and the flow of HIV-infected babies to our refuge in Albany eventually slowed and stopped. Also, infected mothers themselves are now able to take care of their children with HIV longer. Our children at Farano these days more typically have special health and psychological needs not related to HIV, or were sent to us by court order because of neglect and abuse by their parents. A typical stay at Farano is now one to three months, after which some of the children receive court approval to return to their parents, while others are placed by my office into CMS foster homes or in other foster care. There is a strong demand for our new service, a nonresidential program for families in the Albany region with HIV/AIDS.

I find comfort in witnessing these various improvements in the indicators of the quality of life and life expectancy for children with AIDS. Still, I can never forget the harrowing statistics. More than 28,000 children have been orphaned by

AIDS in New York City alone since the epidemic began in 1981. Across the United States, AIDS has orphaned 100,000 children. Worldwide, that number is estimated at a staggering 8.2 million children left motherless because of AIDS. Those figures haunt me.

My grandniece Margie turned five years old this spring, and I celebrated my fifty-second birthday this year. I'm approaching the end of three decades as a Sister of Mercy. The seasons and cycle of life go on. Barbara would have been sixteen years old this August. I can look at her photographs and videotapes now, linger over her drawings and letters, and thank God for the blessing of being given the unexpected opportunity to be a mother to such a wondrous child. At times it all seems like a dream, and I recall the first night I met Barbara and wonder how it all came to be. In those moments, lost in reverie, I feel like I'm back in that movie theater with Amanda and Barbara, watching *Homeward Bound* and seeing the movie of my life unfold. It's a story I never could have dreamed up myself. I've been asked if I would ever consider adopting another child, particularly one with HIV, and I reply that it's not really up to me. Barbara picked me, after all, and I had the easy part—falling in love with a most extraordinary little girl.

I visit the cemetery where Barbara is buried a few times each year. But on warm, sunny days, I would rather walk by a pond with Margie or one of my other grandnieces or grandnephews ... looking for yellow butterflies and remembering Barbara and that place called home.

The Lessons of Barbara

Barbara touched so many lives, she has been commemorated by family, friends, and even strangers in numerous ways. Her classmates at Doane Stuart School planted a tree in her memory. They also helped paint a mural in a study area just off the library with a depiction of Barbara's drawing of a little girl in flight above the clouds and stars with the words, "I had a dream that I could fly." Near that mural, beside a shelf of books, is a lovely maple rocking chair that my family donated to the school in Barbara's memory. In addition, my niece Elizabeth LoGiudice wrote a song for Barbara entitled, "Barbara Can Fly."

Perhaps my favorite commemoration, one that keeps giving, has come from an idea that Barbara's Doane Stuart classmates had after her death. The students collect spare change at school each spring and give the money in Barbara's name to Farano House. They call this annual fund-raising project "Pennies From Heaven." We've used the money to buy extras for the children at Farano, such as playground equipment and new toys. Pennies From Heaven also has paid for special summer day trips for the children.

Barbara and Amanda, best friends in life, remain connected even after their deaths. During an exhibit of the National AIDS Memorial Quilt in Albany in 1998, I participated in a ceremony dedicating panels for Barbara and Amanda. Barbara's panel, designed and created with help from my family, features a butterfly and her favorite Goofy sweatshirt. Amanda's panel has her Minnie Mouse costume, drawings, and a photograph of the two girls. The panels were sewn together and will remain forever linked, a traveling testament to their enduring friendship. Their two panels also are an ongoing piece of AIDS education meant especially to touch youngsters and to remind them that there is nothing to fear about children with AIDS.

Barbara is remembered, too, through her colorful artwork. I took several of her pictures and had them transferred to note cards, which I send to friends and associates. They're known far and wide as "Barbara note cards," and they're used to spread news and love all over the world among people Barbara never met but who, at least for a visual moment, are touched in some small way by her vibrant spirit.

Although Barbara's years with me were few in number, her influence was large and lasting. Even after her death, that special girl, my daughter, remains the center of attention for a group of family and friends. Each year on the anniversary of Barbara's death, June 19, we gather at the home of my brother Joe and his wife, Mary—nieces and nephews, extended family, Sisters of Mercy and former sisters. Father Tony or Father Chris offers a Mass of Remembrance, after which we join together in a meal and recall the lessons Barbara left us by sharing stories, looking at photographs, and watching videos. The anniversary gathering is an important ritual for all of us who were touched by Barbara, a way of keeping her special spirit alive.

I have an ongoing conversation with Barbara, my daughter in heaven. I speak to her in quiet, contemplative moments when I am alone and looking for inspiration or renewed faith. She gives me strength and makes me smile at the memories of our life together. I thank Barbara for all she taught me, for the important lessons I try to carry forward as a way of honoring her. The year before she died, while on retreat at Weston Priory, our special place, a sacred refuge for us both, I wrote a letter to Barbara in which I tried to describe and sum up what she meant to me. I share it now:

My Dear, Sweet, Precious Barbara—

I want to write a letter to you to tell you how much I love you and how important you are to me. You know, it's very difficult to put into words what you feel in your heart, but I want to try.

I remember very clearly those days when I first met you. I would visit at dinnertime, and one day you took my gold bracelet and put it on your head and said, "I am the queen, and you are the princess," and you began to make up a story about a castle and a purple dragon. (You always had a wonderful imagination.) I continued to visit, and I would read you stories and help you get ready for bed. You would hold my face in your little hands and say, "I love you very much," and I would sit in the rocking chair by your crib and hold your hand and sing songs until you went to sleep.

I love you because you teach me once again what it is like to be a child. I know the joy and excitement, the wonder and awe of life when you are so excited about things that you see—the beauty of a butterfly or a sunset or a family of ants working or a spider weaving a web or blowing the dandelion after it goes back to seed. Your delight at jumping in piles of brightly colored leaves (after I raked them) or the beauty of the first snow (sparkling like diamonds, you tell me!). Your wonder and excitement at the simple pleasures in life—God's gifts—have given me a chance to appreciate those wonderful beauties once again, through your eyes.

I love you because you bring me to God. Your innocence, your willingness to trust me in almost anything, your openness to life and eager anticipation of every new event, your faithful love—all bring me closer to God, because you show me, by just loving you, a glimpse of God.

I love you for your determination and perseverance— already you speak about and stand up for what you believe is right.

I love you for your keen, questioning mind. You challenge me to continue to learn, you teach me new things and make me remember other things that I've forgotten.

I love you for your wonderful imagination—the stories

you write and tell are a delight to me.

I love you for your simple trust in me, for your belief that your life is better when I'm with you, for your confidence in me and your emerging confidence in yourself.

I love you for your sense of humor. You say funny things and make me laugh.

I love you for your deep insights. You understand so much more about life and death, and why people do what they do, than many adults.

I love you because you have taught me that each moment is precious—that we should live fully in the present, and not waste it worrying about what might happen in the future.

I love you for your tenderness and understanding of other people when they are hurting. (Like how nice you were to Marilyn when Gram died.)

I love you most of all for the unique, special, wonderful little person that you are. You continue to teach me new things about myself and about life every day. You have made me a better person—more thoughtful and caring and loving. You are a wonderful gift in my life. Words cannot begin to describe how special you are to me. I love you more than anyone else in the world and that love will go on forever.

Mommy

It is important to tell the story of Barbara's life in the hope it will be beneficial in our ongoing efforts in AIDS education. It is only fitting, of course, that Queen Barbara have the last word. Barbara wanted to talk about HIV and AIDS and tell others what she had learned about living with the disease. She was eight years old, and I had discussed with her the details of her illness when Farano House AIDS educator Tracie Killar interviewed her on August 31, 1992. The audiotape interview with Barbara lasted forty-five minutes. Here are excerpts from the transcript:

Q: What would you like to say about HIV?
A: Well, I wish I didn't have it. But you know first when I started talking about it, I didn't have any idea that I had it. I thought I was just safe, clean old me. But then when Mommy told me, I'm like, "You knew! Why didn't you tell me?" I kept asking her, but she explained that she thought I wouldn't understand. I knew there were other kids with HIV, but I didn't think I was one of them.

Q: What did you think when you found out you had HIV?
A: I thought, "Well, I'm safe. I'm never going to get AIDS." But when she told me, I thought, "Man, you didn't tell me." But I know a lot about HIV.

Q: What do you know?
A: HIV is a disease that makes all these viruses in you. And you know what? Amanda has lots of warts under her arms because of HIV. They itch, but she doesn't scratch them a lot. She plays with me, she goes in the water, she never complains about it. What I don't like about HIV is all the medicine. Yeah, I don't like it, especially the Bactrim. You know, I'm going to have to take pills. You know I don't like that 'cause I like the liquid.

Q: How would you tell a friend?

A: I would say, well, um, "I want to say something that I really don't like to say to other people. I'm just not gonna tell other people. I'm just gonna tell you. 'Cause you're my best friend, you're my only friend that I can trust."

Q: How is it keeping the secret?
A: It's hard not telling anyone, especially in school. I really want to spit it out and be done. I guess if the kids knew, they wouldn't play with me. I wish that they would treat me the same way. The parents don't understand about the virus. They think it's horrible. They tell their kids, "Don't play with that girl. You're going to catch it. It's going to be horrible." They're crazy!

Q: What would you tell people?
A: You know what you can tell them, say, "Just because there's someone else in the same school who has HIV with your child doesn't mean that you're going to catch it. There's no other way but blood transfusions and birth, no other way. Kissing, hugging, sharing things. That doesn't make you get it." I would say to the parents, "Don't be afraid … if she kisses me, or shares a spoon or plays with me [it] doesn't matter. She won't get it."

Q: Do you like talking about HIV?
A: Yeah, 'cause then I can get it out of my system.

Q: What kind of pictures would you draw for your HIV book?
A: People playing, kissing and sharing and talking and saying, "Don't think that you're going to get it."

Q: What do you want to be when you grow up?
A: I'll tell you how many keys I'll need. A car key, Mommy's

car key, my house key, Mommy's house key, the school key, June's house key, Amanda's house key—a lot. I want to get a key chain that says my name and Mrs. when I get married.... I want to be a teacher and teach first or second. If they don't have that, I'd like to teach kindergarten. I'll have to go to college.

Afterword

The Story of Our Collaboration

I first met Sister Mary Ann LoGiudice in the fall of 1992. I live in Albany's Pine Hills, a few blocks from North Main Avenue and Community Maternity Services (CMS), the agency for pregnant teens run by Sister Mary Ann under the auspices of Catholic Charities of the Albany Roman Catholic Diocese. I would often drive past or walk along North Main Avenue. There I would see teenage girls—many appeared as innocent and baby-faced as middle-school students— trundling along the street with pregnant bellies or pushing newborns in a stroller. The sight of these kids having kids fascinated me.

I am a feature writer at the Albany *Times Union* in search of human-interest stories. Since teen pregnancy was on the front burner of social issues at the time, I figured this local program would make a compelling feature story. I called

Sister Mary Ann, introduced myself, briefly outlined what I wanted to do, and asked if I could meet with her to discuss further the possibility of a story. When we met in her office, I found her direct and forceful, a straight shooter who let you know where you stood with her. I respected that.

As director of CMS, Sister Mary Ann expressed caution and wariness about the press. She said she wasn't against the idea of a feature story, *per se*, but she had major concerns regarding the confidentiality of her clients and their babies. She was particularly worried about photographs and full names being used, since several of the teenagers had been removed from abusive homes by court order. The court had placed these youthful mothers-to-be in Sister Mary Ann's care, with the stipulation that their whereabouts would remain unknown to their parents or abusers. Sister Mary Ann agreed there was an important human-interest story here, but she was not in any way going to jeopardize the girls through newspaper coverage.

Although I tried to persuade her to allow me full access, Sister Mary Ann remained firm on the ground rules under which I could proceed with my interviews. Only those mothers who wished to participate would be interviewed or photographed (after they signed release forms). Only those who had signed release forms and their babies could be part of the story. Also, these young women would be identified only by first names and photographed in such a way—from the back, at a distance, in dim lighting—that did not reveal their identities. The rest of the clients at CMS, those who for safety or personal reasons did not wish to participate, would not in any way be included in my stories for the *Times Union*.

I agreed to these ground rules and spent more than a week

with the mothers and babies in the CMS residence, which resulted in a three-part series in the *Times Union.*

At the end of each day's reporting, I held a wrap-up interview with Sister Mary Ann in her office. One day, a little girl came running down the hall, sprinted into Sister Mary Ann's office, darted around the desk, hurtled into Sister's lap, threw her arms around the sister and, with a big grin, said, "Mommy! I missed you!"

I'm not sure if I dropped my reporter's notebook, but I'm certain I fumbled with my pen and that my eyebrows arched a bit and my jaw hung lower than usual. I tried to act nonchalant, but Sister Mary Ann noticed my surprise. She introduced Barbara as her daughter. With remarkable poise and confidence for an eight-year-old, Barbara came over to me, shook my hand, said she was pleased to meet me, and then turned the tables. She interviewed *me.* What was I writing in my notebook? What was I asking her mom? Could I put Barbara's name in my story?

She had a captive audience now, and the little girl took advantage of it. Barbara showed me one of her crayon drawings, brought over a couple of toys she kept in her mom's office, and asked me about myself. I told her about my son, Sam, who was two years old at the time. She liked that.

Eventually Sister Mary Ann asked Barbara if she could play in an office down the hall for a few minutes while we finished the interview. Barbara complained and argued for a moment, but after rolling her eyes and heaving a heavy sigh, she did as she was told.

Sister Mary Ann then explained how Barbara had come to Farano House as an orphan with HIV, how she had become Barbara's foster mother, and how she later legally adopted the girl. Sister Mary Ann said only family members and close friends knew that she, a sister, was Barbara's mother. It was not public knowledge. Out of concern for her daughter's privacy and for preserving the confidentiality of Barbara's diagnosis of AIDS, Sister Mary Ann asked for my understanding. "Please do not include Barbara in your story or mention that I have a daughter," Sister Mary Ann said. "She is not part of your story. I hope I can trust your integrity in respecting my request for confidentiality."

I said I understood her concerns and promised that I would not mention Barbara in my articles. However, I added that I thought the story of her and Barbara would be a powerful human-interest story and said that I would like to write it if Sister Mary Ann was ever ready to tell it.

Before I completed my interviews, I saw Barbara a few more times in Sister Mary Ann's office. She was always bubbly and friendly and wanted me to play with her toys and to hear more about my son, Sam.

After publication of my series, which received a strong and positive response, Sister Mary Ann called to thank me for the articles and especially for keeping my promise about not mentioning Barbara. I planted the seed once more about her one day allowing me to write the remarkable story of a Sister of Mercy raising a daughter with AIDS. We said goodbye and parted on good terms.

I noticed the obituary for Barbara in the *Times Union* the following June and sent Sister Mary Ann a note of condolence. After that we lost touch.

Four years later, I received an unexpected phone call from Sister Mary Ann. She said Barbara's death had devastated her and she had grieved for a long time. She said she had just begun to come to terms with the loss and that she was ready to tell Barbara's story if I was ready to hear it. I said I was interested but was finishing another book at the time, a political biography. I said I couldn't give her much time on top of that project, my full-time job at the _Times Union_, and the needs of my wife and two young children. She said she understood. I said I might be able to find an hour or two free each week to speak with her.

That's how this collaboration began. I'd call Sister Mary Ann once a week. It was always late at night—she was busy with meetings and official functions—and usually on Sunday. I'd sit at the computer and type for an hour or two as she poured out the story of her life with Barbara over the phone. This went on for nearly a year, and the pages of notes piled up.

I think it was a kind of therapy for Sister Mary Ann to remember Barbara in this way, by recounting anecdotes and sharing memories that made her laugh and cry. As we went along, we both thought it was a powerful story that would make a good book.

We want to accomplish several things with this narrative. We hope to celebrate the remarkable spirit of Barbara and to commemorate her life. We also think her story can be a positive force in AIDS education. We wish that this story might also serve to inspire readers on their own spiritual journeys, especially those struggling to retain their faith in the face of illness and death. Finally, we want readers to come away with a broader, more complete portrait of religious life and to dispel some old, tired notions about Catholic sisters.

Before looking for a book publisher, we decided to share Barbara's story with the readers of the _Times Union_. Sister

Mary Ann was as direct and forceful as ever when it came to the ground rules governing its publication in the newspaper. We came to a consensus. I reviewed the articles with her before publication, and my eight-part serial narrative appeared in the *Times Union* in May 1998, beginning on Mother's Day. It was called "That Place Called Home," and the series received an overwhelmingly large and positive response from readers—as well as a couple of feature-writing awards.

Encouraged by the warm reaction, we decided to go ahead with our plans for this book. Parts of it first appeared in my *Times Union* series, in different form. In the meantime, we've received interest in making "That Place Called Home" into a television movie.

Through our collaboration we have developed a great amount of trust and respect for each other. Sister Mary Ann has remained the consummate executive director that she is, however, and has had the final say throughout this project. At each juncture she has carefully weighed how best to serve her daughter's memory, while still sharing the moving story of her life with Barbara. She agonized a long time over the TV offer.

In the end we both have a sense that Barbara, who enjoyed the spotlight and being the center of attention, is watching over us as we share her story in various forms. And smiling.

Paul Grondahl
Albany, N.Y.
September 1999